101 Things To Do With Beans

101 Things To Do With Beans

BY
ELIZA CROSS

GIBBS SMITH
TO ENRICH AND INSPIRE HUMANKIND

First Edition
19 18 17 16 15   5 4 3 2

Published by
Gibbs Smith
P.O. Box 667
Layton, Utah 84041

1.800.835.4993 orders
www.gibbs-smith.com

Printed and bound in Korea
Gibbs Smith books are printed on either recycled, 100% post-consumer
waste, FSC-certified papers or on paper produced from sustainable PEFC-
certified forest/controlled wood source. Learn more at www.pefc.org.

Library of Congress Cataloging-in-Publication Data

Cross, Eliza.
   101 things to do with beans / Eliza Cross.
      pages cm
   ISBN 978-1-4236-3949-7
   1. Cooking (Beans) I. Title. II. Title: One hundred and one things to
do with beans. III. Title: One hundred one things to do with beans.
   TX803.B4C76 2015
   641.6'565—dc23
                              2015004778

For Howard Crosslen,

who has bean very, very good to us.

Yum!

**More recipes and tips
at 101yum.com**

CONTENTS

Helpful Hints 9

Soups and Stews

Dinners

Side Dishes

Desserts

HELPFUL HINTS

1. For most beans, 1 pound dried beans = 2 cups dried beans = 5 to 6 cups cooked beans.

2. A 15-ounce can of beans is slightly less than 2 cups of beans, so substitute 1⅞ cups of cooked beans for one can. One pound of dried beans will yield roughly the equivalent of three 15-ounce cans of beans.

3. Before cooking dried beans, spread them in a single layer on a large baking tray and inspect for any small stones or debris. Rinse the beans thoroughly in a fine mesh strainer before cooking.

4. Most dried beans benefit from soaking, which helps begin the process of softening the bean. Very small beans like lentils don't need to be soaked before cooking.

5. Draining and rinsing away the soaking water can help eliminate legumes' complex sugars, which can reduce their gas-causing qualities. Cooking the beans thoroughly, until very tender, breaks down the beans' natural starches; this also helps make them more digestible.

6. Acidic ingredients like vinegar, tomatoes, and tomato juice can slow the cooking time for beans; wait to add these ingredients and the salt until the beans are cooked and tender.

7. Do not boil beans for an extended time, as their skins will break.

8. Smaller legumes like lentils will cook in as little as 1 hour, while larger and harder beans like great Northerns and garbanzo beans may need 2½ to 3 hours of cooking time.

9. Beans are done when they can be easily mashed between two fingers or with a fork. Always test several beans, since they can sometimes cook unevenly.

10. It's a good idea to always allow extra cooking time for dried beans, since their age and moisture content may affect how long it takes for them to become tender.

11. For slow-cooked soups, cook the beans slightly less so they are al dente before adding to the pot; the beans will soften as the soup simmers.

12. Cooked beans can be stored in the refrigerator, covered, for about 3 days.

13. Cooked beans can also be frozen for later use. Cool to room temperature, refrigerate for several hours or overnight, drain, and freeze 1- to 2-cup portions in containers. Thaw the beans overnight in the refrigerator before using.

14. To prevent dried beans from getting hard and stale, store in glass jars with tight-fitting lids.

15. Cooked dried beans generally have a richer flavor and firmer consistency than canned beans.

16. For meals that need to be prepared in a hurry, canned beans are a good alternative to cooked dried beans.

17. Canned beans usually have added salt, so you may need to adjust the salt called for in a recipe. Rinsing and draining canned beans will significantly reduce sodium content.

BASIC BEANS

BASIC COOKED DRIED BEANS

1 pound	**dried beans,** rinsed and picked over
1	**onion,** quartered
1	**bay leaf**
	salt and pepper

The night before or at least 8 hours prior to cooking the beans, pour them into a large pot and cover with water 1 inch above the beans; remove any beans that float to the top. Cover and set aside at room temperature for at least 8 hours or overnight.

Drain and rinse the soaked beans, and transfer back to the pot. Cover with 2 inches of cold water, add the onion and bay leaf, and bring to a boil. Reduce heat, skimming off and discarding any foam on the surface. Cover and simmer, stirring occasionally, until beans are tender, 1 to 3 hours. Discard onion and bay leaf, and season with salt and pepper. Makes 8 servings.

QUICK-SOAKED DRIED BEANS

1 pound	**dried beans,** rinsed and picked over
1	**onion,** quartered
1	**bay leaf**
	salt and pepper

Pour the beans in a large pot and cover with cold water 3 inches above the beans; remove any beans that float to the top. Bring the water to a boil over high heat. Cook the beans for 1 minute. Remove the pot from the heat, cover with a lid and let the beans soak for 1 hour.

Drain and rinse the soaked beans, and transfer back to the pot. Cover with 2 inches of cold water, add the onion and bay leaf, and bring to a boil. Reduce heat, skimming off and discarding any foam on the surface. Cover and simmer, stirring occasionally, until beans are tender, 1 to 3 hours. Discard onion and bay leaf, and season with salt and pepper. Makes 8 servings.

GAS-FREE* ORIEO BEANS

2 ¹/₂ quarts **water**
I pound **dried beans,** rinsed and picked over
I **onion,** quartered
I **bay leaf**
salt and pepper

In a large pot, bring the water to a boil over high heat and add the beans. Boil the beans vigorously for 3 minutes. Remove from heat, cover, and set aside for at least 8 hours or overnight.

Drain the beans, rinsing thoroughly to remove all traces of cooking water, and transfer back to the pot. Cover with water I inch above the beans, add the onion and bay leaf, and bring to a boil. Reduce heat, skimming off and discarding any foam on the surface. Cover and simmer, stirring occasionally, until beans are tender, I to 3 hours. Discard onion and bay leaf, and season with salt and pepper. Makes 8 servings.

*This method for gas-free beans was developed by the California Dry Bean Advisory Board.

OVEN-COOKED DRIED BEANS

I pound	**dried beans,** rinsed and picked over
I teaspoon	**salt**
$^{1}/_{2}$ teaspoon	**pepper**
2 cloves	**garlic,** peeled and minced
I	**bay leaf**

The night before or at least 8 hours prior to cooking the beans, pour them into a large pot and cover with cold water 3 inches above the beans; remove any beans that float to the top. Cover and set aside at room temperature for at least 8 hours or overnight.

Preheat oven to 325 degrees.

Drain and rinse the soaked beans, and transfer them to a 3-quart Dutch oven. Stir in the salt, pepper, garlic, and bay leaf. Cover the beans with water, I inch above the beans. Put the pot on the stove, turn the heat to high, and bring the mixture to a boil.

Remove from the stove and cover. Put the pot in the oven and bake, covered, for 75 minutes. Remove from the oven and check the beans to see if they are soft and tender. If they are too firm, return the pot to the oven and continue checking at 15-minute intervals until done, adding more water to the pot if needed. Remove bay leaf and season with additional salt and pepper if desired. Makes 8 servings.

PRESSURE-COOKED DRIED BEANS

I pound	**dried beans,** rinsed and picked over
I teaspoon	**salt**
I	**small onion,** quartered
I clove	**garlic,** peeled and minced
I	**bay leaf**
I tablespoon	**olive oil**

The night before or at least 8 hours prior to cooking the beans, pour them into a large pot and cover with cold water 3 inches above the beans; remove any beans that float to the top. Cover and set aside at room temperature for at least 8 hours or overnight.

Drain and rinse the soaked beans, and transfer them to a 6- to 8-quart pressure cooker. Add 8 cups of water, salt, onion, garlic, bay leaf, and oil to the pot. Secure the lid according to the instruction manual and turn the heat to high. When the pot reaches high pressure, reduce the heat to medium-low and begin timing the beans according to pressure cooker's instruction manual.

When the time is up, turn off the heat. Allow the pot to cool down and release pressure naturally. Follow pressure cooker's instruction manual to determine when pot is ready to be opened. Carefully unlock and remove the lid, tilting the lid away and allowing any condensation to drip back into the pot. If beans are not quite done, cook over medium heat, uncovered and stirring occasionally, until they reach desired tenderness. Use a slotted spoon to remove the onion and bay leaf. Makes 8 servings.

REFRIED BEANS (FRIJOLES)

1 pound	**dried pinto beans,** rinsed and picked over
6 cups	**water**
2	**onions,** chopped
2 cloves	**garlic,** peeled and minced
2 teaspoons	**salt**
$1/2$ cup	**butter**

The night before or at least 8 hours prior to cooking the beans, pour them into a large pot and cover with cold water 3 inches above the beans; remove any beans that float to the top. Cover and set aside at room temperature for at least 8 hours or overnight.

Drain and rinse the soaked beans, and transfer them back to the pot. Cover with the water and add the onion and garlic. Cook $2^{1}/2$ hours, or until beans are soft. Remove from the heat and drain, reserving the cooking water. Mash beans well with a potato masher. Add salt and some of the cooking water to make a smooth consistency.

Melt the butter in a large skillet over medium heat and add the beans. Cook, mashing and stirring, until butter is incorporated and beans are smooth. Makes 6 servings.

GREEN OR SNAP BEANS

They were once called "string beans," but most fresh snap beans no longer have strings and need only to have their ends trimmed after washing. Beans may be cooked whole, cut in 1-inch lengths, or thinly sliced lengthwise for French-cut beans.

STOVETOP GREEN BEANS

Cook green beans, covered, in a small amount of boiling salted water until crisp-tender:

- 10 to 15 minutes for whole or cut green beans

- 5 to 10 minutes for French-cut green beans

MICROWAVED GREEN BEANS

Place green beans in a casserole dish with 2 tablespoons water. Microwave, covered, on 100 percent power (high) until crisp-tender, stirring once:

- 8 to 12 minutes for whole or cut green beans

- 7 to 10 minutes for French-cut green beans

STEAMED GREEN BEANS

In a steamer over simmering water, cook whole, cut, or French-cut green beans, covered, until crisp-tender:

- 15 to 18 minutes for whole or cut green beans

- 10 to 12 minutes for French-cut green beans

PAN-COOKED GREEN BEANS

Prepare a bowl of ice water and reserve. Bring a large saucepan of salted water to boiling. Add 1 pound whole or cut green beans and cook for 3 to 4 minutes or until crisp-tender. Drain beans and immediately plunge in the ice water. Let the beans sit in ice water for 3 minutes or until cool. Drain well.

In a large skillet heat 1 tablespoon olive oil over medium-high heat. Add beans and cook, stirring occasionally, for 3 to 4 minutes or until tender. Season with salt and pepper. Makes 6 to 8 servings.

SLOW-COOKED "REFRIED" BEANS

3 cups	**dried pinto beans,** rinsed and picked over
1	**onion,** chopped
1 can (4 ounces)	**diced green chiles**
3 cloves	**garlic,** peeled and minced
2 teaspoons	**salt**
1 teaspoon	**pepper**
⅛ teaspoon	**ground cumin**
5 cups	**water**
4 cups	**chicken broth or stock**

Combine the beans, onion, chiles, garlic, salt, pepper, and cumin in a 4-quart slow cooker. Add the water and chicken broth and stir to combine. Cook on high for 8 hours, adding more water as needed. Strain the beans in a large bowl, reserving the liquid. Mash the beans with a potato masher, adding the reserved water as needed to attain a creamy consistency. Adjust seasonings, if needed. Makes 12 servings.

APPETIZERS

GREEN BEAN FRIES

I tablespoon	**salt**
I pound	**fresh green beans,** ends trimmed
I	**egg**
¹/₂ cup	**milk**
2 cups	**seasoned bread crumbs**
I teaspoon	**chili powder**
¹/₂ teaspoon	**garlic powder**
¹/₂ teaspoon	**onion powder**
I cup	**flour**
	vegetable oil for frying
	ranch dressing for dipping

Bring a large saucepan of water to boil. Add the salt and green beans. Cook beans for 3 to 4 minutes or until crisp-tender. Drain beans and transfer to a bowl. Cover with ice water and set aside for 5 minutes. Drain the beans on paper towels.

In a shallow bowl, whisk the egg and milk together. In a separate bowl, mix together the bread crumbs, chili powder, garlic powder, and onion powder. Put the flour in a zip-top bag and toss the green beans with flour to coat, shaking off the excess. Dip the beans into the egg mixture and then into the bread crumbs, coating thoroughly.

Heat the oil in a deep fryer or electric skillet to 375 degrees. Fry beans in batches so they are not touching. Cook until golden brown and crispy, about 2 minutes. Drain on paper towels and serve hot with ranch dressing. Makes 6 servings.

CHICKEN AND BEAN QUESADILLAS

I tablespoon	**vegetable oil**
I	**small onion,** finely chopped
I pound	**boneless skinless chicken breast,** cut in I x $^1/_2$-inch strips
I can (II ounces)	**corn with red and green peppers,** drained
I teaspoon	**chili powder**
$^1/_2$ teaspoon	**ground cumin**
$^1/_2$ teaspoon	**salt**
$^1/_4$ teaspoon	**pepper**
8 (8-inch)	**flour tortillas**
I can (15 ounces)	**refried beans**
I $^1/_2$ cups	**grated Mexican blend cheese**
4 tablespoons	**butter**
$^2/_3$ cup	**sour cream**

In a large skillet, heat the oil over medium-high heat and cook the onion until translucent, about 5 minutes. Add the chicken strips and cook, stirring occasionally, until lightly browned and cooked through. Add the corn, chili powder, cumin, salt, and pepper and cook for I minute. Spread 4 tortillas with $^1/_4$ cup refried beans each (reserve remaining beans for another use). Divide the chicken mixture among the tortillas, and then sprinkle cheese evenly on top of each. Top with the remaining tortillas and press down gently on top to compact the ingredients.

Melt $^1/_2$ tablespoon of the butter in large skillet or griddle over medium heat and cook one side of a quesadilla until golden brown. Lift the quesadilla with a large spatula, and melt another $^1/_2$ tablespoon butter in the skillet. Cook the other side of the quesadilla until golden brown. Repeat with remaining quesadillas. Cut each quesadilla into 6 wedges and serve warm accompanied with sour cream. Makes 24 appetizers.

BEAN AND BEEF TAQUITOS

1/2 pound	**ground beef**
1	**onion,** chopped
1	**jalapeño,** stemmed, seeded, and minced
2 cloves	**garlic,** peeled and minced
1 teaspoon	**ground cumin**
1 teaspoon	**chili powder**
1 cup	**canned refried beans**
1 can (8 ounces)	**tomato sauce**
2 tablespoons	**minced fresh cilantro**
1/2 teaspoon	**salt,** plus additional for sprinkling
1/2 teaspoon	**pepper**
12 (6-inch)	**corn tortillas,** warmed
1	**large egg,** lightly beaten
1/2 cup	**vegetable oil**
	salsa, sour cream, and guacamole, for serving

In a large skillet over medium-high heat, cook the ground beef until no longer pink, about 5 minutes. Spoon beef onto paper towels and drain. Pour out all but 1 tablespoon of drippings from the skillet, and cook the onions over medium heat until lightly browned, about 5 minutes. Add jalapeño, garlic, cumin, and chili powder and cook until fragrant, about 2 minutes. Add refried beans, tomato sauce, 1/4 cup water, cilantro, 1/2 teaspoon salt, and pepper. Stir in drained beef and cook, stirring occasionally, until mixture has thickened, about 10 minutes.

Preheat oven to 425 degrees and line a baking sheet with parchment paper. Brush the top edges of a tortilla with egg. Spoon about 3 tablespoons filling on lower half of the tortilla; roll tightly starting at bottom and place seam-side-down on lined baking sheet. Repeat with remaining tortillas. Lightly brush each taquito with oil and sprinkle with salt. Bake 15 to 18 minutes, turning once, until crisp and golden brown. Serve with salsa, sour cream, and guacamole. Makes 12 taquitos.

CRISPY MINI EMPANADAS

I tablespoon	**olive oil**
¹/₂ pound	**ground turkey**
I	**small red bell pepper,** diced
I	**small onion,** chopped
I clove	**garlic,** peeled and minced
¹/₂ cup	**tomato sauce**
I teaspoon	**ground cumin**
I teaspoon	**chili powder**
I ¹/₂ cups	**grated cheddar cheese**
I can (15 ounces)	**black beans,** rinsed and drained, divided
¹/₄ cup	**chopped fresh cilantro**
2 packages (17.3 ounces each)	**frozen puff pastry** (4 sheets), thawed
I	**egg,** whisked with I tablespoon water
	sour cream and salsa, for serving

Preheat oven to 375 degrees and grease two baking sheets. In a large skillet over medium-high heat, heat the oil until it shimmers and add the turkey. Cook, stirring occasionally, for 5 to 7 minutes, or until thoroughly cooked. Add the red pepper, onion, and garlic and cook until tender. Stir in the tomato sauce, cumin, and chili powder and reduce heat to low. Cook for 5 minutes. Remove from the heat and cool for 5 minutes. Stir in the cheese, I cup beans, and the cilantro. Cover and reserve.

Unfold each pastry sheet on a lightly floured surface, roll into a 12 x 16-inch rectangle, and cut into 10 (2¹/₂-inch) rounds, making 40 rounds total. Spoon I teaspoon of the bean mixture on half of each pastry circle. Brush the edges of the pastry with water. Fold the pastry over the filling and crimp with a fork to seal. Arrange the pastries I inch apart on baking sheets, and brush each with the egg mixture. Bake for 15 minutes, or until the pastries are golden brown. Remove the pastries from the baking sheets and let cool on wire racks for 10 minutes. Serve the pastries with the sour cream, salsa, and remaining beans. Makes 40 appetizers.

ULTIMATE NACHOS

1 pound	**ground beef**
1	**onion,** finely diced
	salt and pepper
1/3 cup	**medium salsa**
3 ounces	**cream cheese,** cut in 1-inch cubes
1 can (15 ounces)	**refried beans**
1 bag (13 ounces)	**tortilla chips**
2 cups	**grated cheddar cheese**
1 cup	**guacamole**
1/2 cup	**sour cream**
1	**large tomato,** chopped
4	**green onions,** minced
1 can (2.25 ounces)	**sliced black olives**

Preheat oven to 350 degrees and line a baking sheet with foil.

In a large skillet, cook the ground beef and onion over medium heat, breaking up the beef with a spoon and cooking until beef starts to brown and onion is translucent. Season to taste with salt and pepper and drain off grease. Add the salsa and cook for 3 minutes, or until mixture starts to thicken. Remove from heat, cover, and keep warm.

Put the cream cheese in a medium glass dish and microwave for 20 seconds, or until softened. Add the refried beans and stir until completely combined.

Arrange the chips evenly on the prepared baking sheet. Spread the bean mixture over the chips. Layer with half of the cheese, the ground beef mixture, and remaining cheese. Bake nachos until cheese melts and filling is bubbly, about 6 to 8 minutes. Remove from oven and top with dollops of guacamole and sour cream. Sprinkle with chopped tomato, green onions, and black olives. Makes 6 servings.

8-LAYER DIP

I pound	**ground beef**
I package (I ounce)	**taco seasoning mix,** divided
I can (15 ounces)	**refried beans**
I can (10 ounces)	**diced tomatoes and green chiles,** drained, liquid reserved
I pint	**sour cream**
I package (8 ounces)	**cream cheese,** softened
I ½ cups	**prepared guacamole**
I jar (16 ounces)	**salsa**
4	**green onions,** chopped
2 cups	**grated cheddar cheese**
I can (6 ounces)	**sliced black olives,** drained
	tortilla chips

Cook ground beef in a skillet over medium-high heat until cooked through and no longer pink, stirring occasionally; drain and return to the skillet. Add half the taco seasoning mix and stir to combine; reserve.

In a medium bowl, blend refried beans, the liquid from the tomatoes and green chiles, and the remaining taco seasoning mix; stir until well blended and spread the mixture in the bottom of a 9 x 13-inch baking dish. Sprinkle the ground beef mixture evenly on top.

Mix the sour cream and cream cheese in a medium bowl and spread over the ground beef layer. Spread evenly with the guacamole. Pour the salsa evenly over the guacamole and top with the drained tomatoes and green chiles. Sprinkle evenly with the green onions and sprinkle the cheddar cheese on top. Garnish with black olives. Serve with tortilla chips. Makes 12 servings.

BABY TOSTADAS

36	**"scoop" style tortilla chips**
1 cup	**refried beans** (from 15-ounce can)
1 cup	**refrigerated guacamole**
1 cup	**shredded cooked chicken**
1/2 cup	**shredded lettuce**
1/2 cup	**salsa**
3 tablespoons	**chopped fresh cilantro**

Arrange the tortilla chips on a large serving platter. In a small saucepan over medium heat, cook the refried beans, stirring occasionally, until heated through. Spread each chip with 1 heaping teaspoon refried beans. Top with 1 heaping teaspoon guacamole and 1 heaping teaspoon chicken. Divide the lettuce evenly among the appetizers and drizzle with the salsa. Sprinkle with the cilantro and serve at once. Makes 36 appetizers.

EASY CREAMY HUMMUS DIP

1 can (15 ounces)	**garbanzo beans,** rinsed and drained
1 tablespoon	**lemon juice**
1 clove	**garlic,** peeled and minced
2 tablespoons	**sesame seeds**
1/4 cup	**olive oil,** plus more as needed
	salt and pepper
	fresh vegetables or pita chips

Combine the beans, lemon juice, garlic, and sesame seeds in a food processor and process for 1 minute; scrape down the sides of the bowl and pulse to blend. With the motor running, slowly add the olive oil until ingredients are blended into a smooth spread, adding more if needed. Season to taste with salt and pepper. Use at once or refrigerate up to 2 days. Serve with fresh vegetables or pita chips. Makes about 2 1/2 cups.

ASIAN SOYBEAN HUMMUS

I can (15 ounces)	**cannellini beans,** rinsed and drained
1 ½ cups	**shelled, cooked fresh or frozen edamame** (green soybeans)
2 cloves	**garlic,** peeled and chopped
¼ cup	**water,** plus more as needed
3 tablespoons	**lemon juice**
2 tablespoons	**olive oil**
I teaspoon	**salt**
¼ teaspoon	**sesame oil**
¼ teaspoon	**pepper**
2 tablespoons	**coarsely chopped fresh cilantro**
1 ½ teaspoons	**sesame seeds**
	fresh vegetables for dipping

Place the cannellini beans, edamame, garlic, water, lemon juice, olive oil, salt, sesame oil, and pepper in a food processor fitted with a blade attachment. Process until smooth. Scrape down the sides and process again. If the dip is too thick, pulse in more water, a tablespoon at a time, until the desired consistency is reached.

Transfer to a medium serving bowl, add the cilantro, and stir to combine. Sprinkle with sesame seeds and serve with assorted fresh vegetables. Makes 8 servings.

ITALIAN WHITE BEAN SPREAD

1 can (15 ounces)	**cannellini beans,** rinsed and drained
1 clove	**garlic,** peeled and roughly chopped
1 1/2 teaspoons	**lemon juice**
2 tablespoons	**olive oil,** plus more as needed
1/2 teaspoon	**salt**
1/4 teaspoon	**pepper**
	garlic bagel chips or crackers

Combine the beans, garlic, and lemon juice in a food processor or blender. With the motor running, slowly add the olive oil and process until smooth, adding more if needed. Scrape down the sides, add the salt and pepper, and process again. Taste and adjust seasonings if necessary. Spoon into a bowl and serve warm with garlic bagel chips or crackers. Makes 4 servings.

BLACK BEAN SALSA

2	**medium, ripe avocados,** peeled and diced
2 tablespoons	**lime juice**
I can (15 ounces)	**black beans,** rinsed and drained
I can (15 ounces)	**whole kernel corn,** drained
I	**medium red bell pepper,** chopped
2	**green onions,** chopped
2 tablespoons	**minced fresh cilantro**
3 cloves	**garlic,** peeled and minced
2 tablespoons	**olive oil**
I teaspoon	**red wine vinegar**
1/2 teaspoon	**salt**
1/4 teaspoon	**pepper**
	tortilla chips

In a medium bowl, combine the avocados and lime juice; let stand, stirring gently several times, for 10 minutes. In a large bowl, combine the beans, corn, red pepper, green onions, cilantro, and garlic.

In a small bowl, whisk together the oil, vinegar, salt, and pepper. Drizzle over bean mixture; toss to coat. Gently fold in the avocado mixture. Cover and refrigerate for at least 2 hours or until chilled. Serve with tortilla chips. Makes 8 servings.

LAYERED ANTIPASTO DIP

1 can (15 ounces)	**great Northern beans,** rinsed and drained
¼ cup	**grated Parmesan cheese**
¼ cup	**Italian salad dressing**
¼ pound	**thick-sliced pepperoni,** finely chopped
½ cup	**chopped and drained roasted red peppers**
¾ cup	**grated Italian cheese blend**
1 tablespoon	**chopped fresh oregano** **assorted crackers**

Preheat oven to 350 degrees.

Place beans, Parmesan cheese, and salad dressing in food processor bowl fitted with a metal blade; process until smooth. Spread mixture in a 9-inch glass pie pan. Top with pepperoni, peppers, cheese, and oregano. Cover with foil.

Bake for 10 minutes, or until cheese is melted and mixture is bubbling. Serve with crackers. Makes 8 servings.

CREAMY HOT BLACK BEAN DIP

I tablespoon	**olive oil**
2 tablespoons	**chopped onions**
I can (4 ounces)	**diced green chiles**
I	**tomato,** diced
I teaspoon	**chili powder**
$^{1}/_{2}$ teaspoon	**salt**
I can (15 ounces)	**black beans with jalapeños**
I cup	**grated cheddar cheese**
$^{1}/_{2}$ cup	**grated Monterey Jack cheese**
4 ounces	**cream cheese,** diced
	baked flour tortilla chips
	or corn chips

Heat the olive oil in a skillet over medium heat and cook the onions until tender, about 5 minutes. Add the chiles, tomato, chili powder, and salt and cook for 5 minutes, stirring occasionally.

Spoon half of the black beans with some of the liquid from the can into the bowl of a food processor and process until smooth. Scrape down the sides and process again. Add the puréed bean mixture and remaining beans to the onion mixture and cook until hot. Add the cheddar and Monterey Jack cheeses and cream cheese. Cook, stirring constantly, until hot and bubbling. Transfer to a serving dish and serve hot with tortilla or corn chips. Makes 4 servings.

WHITE BEAN RED PEPPER DIP

1 can (15 ounces)	**white cannellini or navy beans,** rinsed and drained
1 jar (12 ounces)	**roasted red peppers,** drained
4 ounces	**cream cheese,** softened
1 clove	**garlic,** peeled and minced
1 tablespoon	**lemon juice**
	salt and pepper
	pita chips

Purée the ingredients, except pita chips, in a food processor until smooth. Season with salt and pepper to taste and serve with pita chips. Makes 8 servings.

BEAN AND CORN CON QUESO

1 tablespoon	**butter**
1/2 cup	**chopped onions**
1 tablespoon	**flour**
1 cup	**milk**
1 teaspoon	**ground cumin**
1 teaspoon	**salt**
1/8 teaspoon	**cayenne pepper**
1 can (15 ounces)	**spicy whole pinto beans,** drained
1 can (11 ounces)	**corn with red and green peppers,** drained
3/4 cup	**grated cheddar cheese**
	corn chips

Melt butter in a large saucepan over medium heat. Add the onions and cook, stirring occasionally, until translucent. Reduce heat to low and sprinkle with the flour. Cook for 1 minute, stirring constantly. Slowly add the milk, stirring constantly, and cook until sauce starts to thicken. Stir in the cumin, salt, and cayenne pepper.

Add the beans and corn and continue cooking just until mixture starts to bubble around the edges. Add the cheese and cook, stirring, just until cheese is melted. Serve warm with corn chips. Makes 6 servings.

GARLIC CHILE BACON EDAMAME

I pound	**whole frozen edamame** (green soybeans)
$^1/_2$ pound	**bacon,** chopped in $^1/_4$-inch pieces
4 to 6 cloves	**garlic,** peeled and finely minced
2 tablespoons	**soy sauce**
2 teaspoons	**crushed red chile peppers**

Fill a large pot with water and heat to boiling. Cook the frozen edamame in the pods until tender, about 5 minutes; drain.

In a large skillet, cook the bacon over medium heat until crispy. Use a slotted spoon to remove the bacon and drain on paper towels, reserving 2 tablespoons drippings. Heat the drippings over medium-high heat and sauté the garlic until lightly golden, I to 2 minutes. Add the whole edamame and stir until coated, about 2 minutes. Add the soy sauce and continue cooking and stirring for I minute. Remove from the heat and sprinkle with the bacon and chile peppers, stirring to coat. Transfer the edamame to a platter and serve warm. (The edamame is eaten by gently pulling a pod through the teeth, discarding the empty pod.) Makes 4 servings.

EASY REFRIGERATOR DILLY BEANS

1 bunch	**fresh dill**
2 cloves	**garlic,** peeled
1 teaspoon	**yellow mustard seeds**
1 teaspoon	**dill seeds**
$1/4$ teaspoon	**cayenne pepper**
1 pound	**fresh green beans,** ends trimmed
1 $1/3$ cup	**cider vinegar**
1 $1/3$ cup	**water**
2 tablespoons	**kosher salt**
1 tablespoon	**sugar**

Use tongs to place 2 (1-pint) canning jars and lids in a pot of boiling water; heat for 1 minute. Lift out, drain, and place on the counter. Divide the fresh dill, garlic, mustard seeds, dill seeds, and cayenne between the 2 jars. Pack the raw green beans in lengthwise.

In a small saucepan, combine the vinegar, water, salt, and sugar and bring to a boil over high heat, stirring until salt and sugar dissolve.

Pour the boiling liquid over the green beans, leaving $1/2$ inch of space at the top. Screw on the lid and let the jars cool on a wire rack to room temperature. Refrigerate for 2 days before serving, and eat within 2 weeks. Makes 2 pints or 8 servings.

CRISPY ROASTED CHICKPEAS

I teaspoon	**ground cumin**
I teaspoon	**chili powder**
¹/₂ teaspoon	**salt**
¹/₄ teaspoon	**cayenne pepper** (or substitute black pepper)
2 cans (15 ounces each)	**garbanzo beans,** rinsed and drained
2 tablespoons	**olive oil**

Preheat the oven to 350 degrees.

Combine the cumin, chili powder, salt, and cayenne or pepper in a small bowl. Spread the beans on several layers of paper towels and cover with another layer, blotting until completely dry. Remove and discard any loosened skins from the beans.

Drizzle the olive oil over the beans and spread evenly in a rimmed cookie sheet. Bake for 30 minutes, stirring several times during cooking. Remove the beans from the oven, stir, and cool in the pan for 5 minutes. Return to the oven and cook for about 15 to 20 minutes, or until beans are golden and crunchy. Remove from the oven and sprinkle with the spice blend, stirring to coat evenly. Serve warm or at room temperature. Makes 8 servings.

SALADS

MARINATED BEAN AND ARTICHOKE SALAD

I can (15 ounces)	**kidney beans,** rinsed and drained
I can (15 ounces)	**cut green beans,** drained
I jar (6.5 ounces)	**marinated artichoke hearts,** with liquid
1/2 cup	**chopped green bell pepper**
I	**small red onion,** chopped
1/3 cup	**Italian salad dressing**
	salt and pepper

In a large bowl, toss together all the ingredients. Season to taste with salt and pepper, cover, and refrigerate for at least 2 hours or overnight. Stir before serving. Makes 6 to 8 servings.

FRENCH GREEN BEAN SALAD

I package (2 ounces)	**slivered almonds** (about $1/2$ cup)
$1/2$ teaspoon	**salt**
I package (16 ounces)	**frozen French-style green beans**
6	**bacon strips**
$1/2$ cup	**chopped onion**
$1/2$ cup	**ranch salad dressing**

Heat the oven to 350 degrees and spread the almonds on a baking sheet. Bake for about 5 minutes, or just until lightly browned. Sprinkle with salt and cool to room temperature.

Bring a large pan of salted water to a boil over medium-high heat. Add green beans and cook until tender, 3 to 4 minutes. Transfer to a colander, rinse with cool water, and drain; reserve. In a large skillet, cook the bacon until brown and crispy; drain on paper towels and crumble when cool. Put the bacon crumbles in a covered container and refrigerate.

Drain all but 2 teaspoons drippings from the pan and cook the onion in the drippings over medium heat until just starting to brown, about 5 minutes. In a medium serving bowl, combine the green beans, onion, and ranch dressing; cover and chill for 2 hours or overnight. Just before serving, add the toasted almonds and bacon crumbles and stir to combine. Makes 6 servings.

SUMMER TOMATO BEAN SALAD

3 cups	**chopped romaine lettuce leaves**
1 can (15 ounces)	**kidney beans,** rinsed and drained
2	**large ripe tomatoes,** seeded and diced
2 stalks	**celery,** sliced
4	**green onions,** sliced
$1/2$ cup	**mayonnaise**
$1/4$ cup	**ranch salad dressing**
1 teaspoon	**dill weed**
$1/4$ teaspoon	**garlic powder**

In a serving bowl, combine the lettuce, beans, tomatoes, celery, and green onions. In a small bowl, combine the mayonnaise, ranch dressing, dill, and garlic powder. Pour over vegetables and stir gently to combine. Makes 6 servings.

ITALIAN TORTELLINI AND BEAN SALAD

I package (9 ounces)	**refrigerated spinach tortellini**
2 cups	**fresh broccoli florets**
¹/₂	**large red onion,** thinly sliced
I cup	**canned garbanzo beans or chickpeas,** rinsed and drained
I cup	**canned red kidney beans,** rinsed and drained
I cup	**canned white kidney beans or cannellini beans,** rinsed and drained
I can (6 ounces)	**pitted ripe olives,** drained
I jar (4 ounces)	**diced pimientos**
I cup	**Italian salad dressing**
24	**cherry tomatoes,** halved
¹/₄ cup	**grated Parmesan cheese**
¹/₄ cup	**finely chopped fresh basil or Italian parsley**

Prepare tortellini according to package directions; drain and place in a serving bowl. Add broccoli, onion, beans, olives, and pimientos. Drizzle the dressing over the salad and toss gently. Cover and refrigerate for at least 8 hours.

Just before serving, stir in tomatoes and sprinkle with Parmesan and basil or parsley. Makes 10 to 12 servings.

WHITE BEAN
AND TUNA SALAD

2 cans (5 ounces each)	**light tuna,** drained
I can (I5 ounces)	**white beans,** drained and rinsed
I	**small red bell pepper,** seeded and diced
I	**tomato,** seeded and diced
2 large stalks	**celery,** diced
I tablespoon	**olive oil**
2 tablespoons	**lemon juice**
	salt and pepper
3 cups	**mixed salad greens**
I tablespoon	**minced parsley**

Combine the tuna, beans, bell pepper, tomato, and celery in a medium bowl. Drizzle with the olive oil and lemon juice and stir gently. Cover and chill in the refrigerator for at least 4 hours. Season with salt and pepper.

Divide the mixed greens among 6 chilled salad plates and mound the salad on top of each plate. Garnish with minced parsley. Makes 6 servings.

ANTIPASTO SALAD

3 cups	**spiral or rotini pasta noodles**
2 cups	**fresh broccoli florets**
I can (15 ounces)	**dark red kidney beans,** rinsed and drained
$^1/_2$ pound	**cherry tomatoes,** halved
$^1/_4$ pound	**thinly sliced salami,** cut in $^1/_2$-inch strips
I	**medium green bell pepper,** chopped
$^1/_2$	**medium red onion,** chopped and rinsed
$^1/_2$ cup	**pitted black or green olives,** halved
$^3/_4$ cup	**Italian dressing**
$^1/_2$ cup (2 ounces)	**freshly grated Parmesan cheese**
$^1/_2$ teaspoon	**pepper**
3 cloves	**garlic,** peeled and minced

Heat a large pot of water over high heat to boiling and cook the pasta as directed on package, adding broccoli during last 3 minutes of cook time; drain, rinse with cool water, and drain again.

Transfer the mixture to a large serving bowl and add the beans, cherry tomatoes, salami, bell pepper, onion, and olives; stir to combine.

In a small bowl whisk together the Italian dressing, Parmesan cheese, black pepper, and garlic. Drizzle dressing over salad, tossing gently to mix. Cover and refrigerate at least 2 hours. Stir before serving. Makes 6 servings.

FRENCH SALAD NICOISE

½ pound	**red potatoes,** scrubbed and cut in half
1 pound	**fresh green beans,** ends trimmed
2 cans (5 ounces each)	**tuna,** drained
½ teaspoon	**salt**
¼ teaspoon	**pepper**
1 head	**butter lettuce,** washed, dried, and torn into bite-size pieces
2	**medium tomatoes,** each cut into 8 wedges
2	**hard-cooked eggs,** each cut into 4 wedges
½ cup	**pitted ripe olives**
¾ cup	**vinaigrette salad dressing**
2 tablespoons	**chopped fresh basil**

Bring a large pot of water to a boil over high heat and cook the potatoes until tender. Use a slotted spoon to remove the potatoes to a colander; drain and reserve. Add the green beans to the water and cook until crisp-tender, about 5 minutes. Drain, rinse with cold water, and drain again. Refrigerate the potatoes and beans for 2 hours.

Put the tuna in a small bowl and sprinkle with salt and pepper; use a fork to mix until well combined. Line 4 chilled salad plates with butter lettuce. Arrange the green beans, potatoes, tomatoes, and eggs around edges of plates. Mound the tuna in the center and garnish with the olives. In a small bowl, whisk together the vinaigrette and basil until combined; drizzle over the salads. Makes 4 servings.

YELLOW AND GREEN SALAD WITH TOMATO DRESSING

³/₄ pound	**fresh yellow beans,** ends trimmed
³/₄ pound	**fresh green beans,** ends trimmed
2	**large tomatoes,** finely chopped
I tablespoon	**balsamic vinegar**
2 teaspoons	**olive oil**
¹/₂ teaspoon	**salt**
¹/₄ teaspoon	**pepper**
¹/₂ cup	**fresh basil leaves,** finely sliced
¹/₂ cup	**grated Parmesan cheese**

In a large pot of boiling water, cook the beans over high heat until crisp-tender, about 5 minutes. Drain and rinse with cold water.

Whisk together the tomatoes, vinegar, oil, salt, and pepper in a small bowl. Divide the beans evenly among 8 plates and drizzle with the dressing. Sprinkle each serving with I tablespoon sliced basil and I tablespoon cheese. Makes 8 servings.

CHICKPEA CORN SALAD WITH LIME DRESSING

3 large or 4 small	**ears fresh corn,** shucked, or 1 package (16 ounces) frozen corn
1/4 cup plus 1 tablespoon	**olive oil,** divided
1	**jalapeño,** seeded and minced
1/4 cup	**finely chopped red onion**
2 cloves	**garlic,** peeled and minced
2 cans (15 ounces each)	**garbanzo beans,** rinsed and drained
2	**tomatoes,** diced
1	**small green bell pepper,** seeded and diced
3 tablespoons	**lime juice**
2 teaspoons	**ground cumin**
1/2 teaspoon	**salt**
	pepper

Cook the corn in a pot of boiling water over medium-high heat until tender, about 4 minutes. Drain and cool the corn. Use a sharp serrated knife to cut the kernels from the cobs. (If using frozen corn, cook according to package directions.) Reserve.

In a large skillet over medium heat, heat 1 tablespoon of the olive oil and sauté the jalapeño, onion, and garlic until tender. Remove from heat and reserve.

In a serving bowl, combine the corn, garbanzo beans, tomatoes, green pepper, and onion mixture.

In a small bowl, whisk together the remaining 1/4 cup olive oil, lime juice, cumin, and salt. Drizzle over the salad and stir gently. Season with salt and pepper to taste. Makes 8 servings.

WHITE BEAN AND AVOCADO SALAD

I can (15 ounces)	**white beans,** rinsed and drained
I	**avocado,** peeled and cut in $1/2$-inch cubes
I	**medium tomato,** chopped
$1/4$ cup	**chopped sweet onion**
3 tablespoons	**olive oil**
$1/4$ cup	**lemon juice**
$1/2$ teaspoon	**dry mustard**
$1/2$ teaspoon	**dried basil**
$1/4$ teaspoon	**garlic powder**
$1/4$ teaspoon	**salt**
$1/4$ teaspoon	**pepper**
4 leaves	**butter lettuce**
I tablespoon	**chopped Italian parsley**

In a medium bowl, combine the beans, avocado, tomato, and onion and stir gently. In a small bowl, whisk together the olive oil, lemon juice, mustard, basil, garlic powder, salt, and pepper until well combined. Drizzle over the salad and toss gently. Cover and refrigerate for at least 2 hours before serving.

Arrange a lettuce leaf on each of 4 chilled salad plates and divide the salad evenly among the plates; sprinkle with chopped parsley. Makes 4 servings.

YELLOW BEAN SALAD WITH BASIL VINAIGRETTE

1 pound	**fresh yellow beans** (or substitute green beans), ends trimmed
1/2 cup	**fresh basil leaves,** plus extra for garnish
2 cloves	**garlic,** peeled and chopped
2 tablespoons	**olive oil**
2 tablespoons	**balsamic or red wine vinegar**
2 teaspoons	**Dijon mustard**
1/2 teaspoon	**salt**
1/2 teaspoon	**pepper**

In a large pot of boiling water, cook the beans over high heat until crisp-tender, about 5 minutes. Drain the beans, rinsing with cold water to stop cooking. Transfer to a medium serving dish, cover, and refrigerate for 1 hour.

Combine the basil, garlic, oil, vinegar, mustard, salt, and pepper in a food processor and pulse several times until the mixture is blended. Scrape down the sides and pulse again. Drizzle the dressing over the chilled beans and toss gently to coat. Garnish with basil leaves. Makes 4 to 6 servings.

SPINACH AND BLACK-EYED-PEA SALAD

2 tablespoons	**finely chopped fresh basil leaves**
³/₄ cup	**ranch dressing**
2 cans (15 ounces each)	**black-eyed peas,** rinsed and drained
¹/₄ cup	**diced red onion**
2 stalks	**celery,** thinly sliced
2 tablespoons	**chopped fresh chives**
4 cups	**baby spinach**
	salt and pepper
3 slices	**bacon,** cooked, drained and crumbled

In a small bowl, gently stir together the chopped basil and ranch dressing; reserve.

In a salad bowl, combine black-eyed peas, onion, celery, and chives. Drizzle half of the dressing over the mixture and stir gently to blend. Add spinach, drizzle with remaining dressing, and toss to coat. Season with salt and pepper and garnish with crumbled bacon. Makes 6 servings.

SPROUTS AND PEAS SALAD

1 package (16 ounces)	**frozen black-eyed peas**
1 package (16 ounces)	**frozen peas**
1/2 pound	**fresh bean sprouts**
1/2	**small red onion,** chopped
1/4 cup	**olive oil**
2 tablespoons	**apple cider vinegar**
2 cloves	**garlic,** peeled and minced
	salt and pepper
1 pint	**ripe grape or cherry tomatoes,** halved
1/4 pound	**fresh alfalfa sprouts**

Cook the black-eyed peas and peas according to package directions and drain. Combine in a large serving bowl, cover, and refrigerate for at least 2 hours.

Remove from the refrigerator and add the bean sprouts and onion; toss gently to combine. In a small bowl, whisk together the oil, vinegar, and garlic until blended. Drizzle the dressing over the salad and toss gently to combine. Season with salt and pepper. Add the cherry tomatoes just before serving and stir gently. Garnish with alfalfa sprouts. Makes 10 to 12 servings.

BEST TACO SALAD

1 pound	**lean ground beef**
1 package (1.25 ounces)	**taco seasoning mix**
1 can (15 ounces)	**kidney beans,** rinsed and drained
2	**ripe tomatoes,** diced
2 cups	**grated Mexican blend cheese**
4	**green onions,** chopped
1 head	**iceberg lettuce,** chopped
1 cup	**Catalina, ranch, or Italian salad dressing**
1 bag (13 ounces)	**plain or taco-flavored tortilla chips**
1 cup	**salsa**
1 cup	**sour cream**

In a large skillet, brown the ground beef over medium-high heat. Drain the grease and add the taco seasoning mix, beans, and ¼ cup water. Cook over medium heat, stirring, until slightly thickened, about 5 minutes. Remove from heat and cool to room temperature. Transfer to a covered container and refrigerate for at least 2 hours.

In a large serving bowl, combine the ground beef mixture, tomatoes, cheese, green onions, and lettuce in a large bowl. Add the salad dressing and mix well. Crumble the tortilla chips in bite-sized pieces, add to the salad, and toss. Serve with salsa and sour cream. Makes 6 servings.

LAYERED POTLUCK SALAD

I head	**romaine lettuce,** chopped
1/2 cup	**chopped celery**
I can (8 ounces)	**sliced water chestnuts,** drained and chopped
2 cups	**grated cheddar cheese**
I bunch	**green onions,** chopped
I can (15 ounces)	**garbanzo beans,** rinsed and drained
I package (16 ounces)	**frozen green peas,** partially thawed
I cup	**mayonnaise**
1/2 cup	**sour cream**
I teaspoon	**sugar**
1/2 teaspoon	**seasoning salt**
1/4 teaspoon	**garlic powder**
1/4 teaspoon	**pepper**
1/2 pound	**bacon,** cooked and crumbled
4	**hard-boiled eggs,** peeled and chopped
I	**large tomato,** chopped and drained

In a clear glass serving bowl, layer the lettuce, celery, water chestnuts, cheese, green onions, garbanzo beans, and peas.

In a medium bowl, combine the mayonnaise, sour cream, sugar, seasoning salt, garlic powder, and pepper and stir until smooth. Spread evenly over the salad to the edge of the bowl. Cover and refrigerate overnight.

Remove the salad from the refrigerator and top with the crumbled bacon, eggs, and tomato. Just before serving, toss the salad to incorporate the dressing. Makes 8 servings.

ROASTED GREEN BEAN SALAD WITH PISTACHIOS

⅓ cup	**shelled pistachio nuts,** roughly chopped
1 pound	**fresh green beans,** ends trimmed
4 tablespoons	**olive oil,** divided
2 cloves	**garlic,** peeled and minced
¼ teaspoon	**salt**
2 tablespoons	**wine vinegar**
	pepper
¼ cup	**grated Parmesan cheese**

Preheat oven to 350 degrees.

Spread the pistachios on a baking sheet and bake for 4 to 5 minutes or until fragrant, stirring halfway through cooking time. Remove from oven, cool, and reserve.

Increase the oven heat to 425 degrees and arrange a rack on the top shelf.

In a medium bowl, toss the beans with 1 tablespoon olive oil. Spread in single layer on a baking sheet and bake for 20 minutes or until beans are tender, stirring halfway through cooking time. Remove from oven and cool to room temperature. Transfer the beans to a serving dish and reserve.

In a small bowl, use the back of a spoon to mash the garlic with ¼ teaspoon salt. Whisk in the vinegar and remaining 3 tablespoons olive oil. Drizzle the dressing over the beans and season to taste with salt and pepper. Sprinkle the toasted pistachio nuts and Parmesan cheese on top. Makes 4 to 6 servings.

ZESTY GREEN BEAN
AND CUCUMBER SALAD

I	**cucumber,** peeled and cut in ¹/₄-inch slices
¹/₂ teaspoon	**salt**
I tablespoon	**olive oil**
I tablespoons	**red wine vinegar**
I teaspoon	**honey**
¹/₂ pound	**fresh green beans,** ends trimmed
¹/₄ cup	**finely sliced red onion**
I	**Anaheim pepper,** seeded and finely chopped
2 tablespoons	**chopped fresh cilantro**

Fill a large pot or bowl ²/₃ full with ice and water; reserve. Cut the cucumber slices in half and arrange on paper towels. Sprinkle with salt and reserve. In a small bowl, whisk together the olive oil, vinegar, and honey and reserve.

In a large pot of boiling water, cook the beans over high heat until crisp-tender, about 5 minutes. Drain the beans, rinse with cool water, and pour in the ice water to stop cooking. After 3 minutes, drain the beans and cut in I-inch pieces; transfer to a serving bowl. Add the cucumber, red onion, and pepper and stir gently. Drizzle with the dressing and stir to combine. Cover and refrigerate for 2 hours. Sprinkle with cilantro. Makes 6 servings.

CHOPPED SALAD

1/2 head	**romaine lettuce,** chopped
1/2 head	**iceberg lettuce,** chopped
2 tablespoons	**thinly sliced fresh basil**
1 can (15 ounces)	**garbanzo beans,** rinsed and drained
1	**medium tomato,** cored and cut into 1/4-inch dice
1 can (4.25 ounces)	**sliced black olives,** drained
1	**avocado,** peeled and diced
1/3 to 1/2 cup	**creamy Italian dressing**

Combine the romaine and iceberg lettuces and basil in a large bowl and toss to combine. Add the garbanzo beans, tomato, olives, and avocado and toss gently. Drizzle with 1/3 cup of the dressing and toss gently. Add additional dressing if needed; toss and serve. Makes 4 servings.

SOUPS AND STEWS

ITALIAN CHICKPEA AND VEGETABLE STEW

1/4 cup	**olive oil**
2	**medium onions,** chopped
2 cloves	**garlic,** peeled and minced
3	**medium potatoes,** peeled and cut in 1/2-inch cubes
1 can (15 ounces)	**garbanzo beans,** rinsed and drained
2	**large, ripe tomatoes,** chopped
4 cups	**chicken broth**
1 teaspoon	**Italian seasoning blend**
1 1/2 tablespoons	**tomato paste**
1/2 teaspoon	**salt**
1/2 teaspoon	**pepper**

Heat oil in a 3-quart soup pot or Dutch oven over medium heat, and sauté onions until transparent. Add the garlic and cook until lightly browned. Add the potatoes, stirring occasionally, and cook until lightly browned. Add the garbanzo beans and tomatoes and stir to combine.

In a small bowl, combine the broth with the Italian seasoning, tomato paste, salt, and pepper. Add to garbanzo mixture and stir to combine. Bring to a boil and reduce heat to medium-low. Simmer, covered, until potatoes are tender, about 25 minutes. Makes 4 servings.

CREAMY WHITE BEAN CHOWDER

1 1/2 cups	**dried white beans (navy, Michigan or great Northern),** rinsed
6 cups	**water**
6 tablespoons	**butter**
1 teaspoon	**finely chopped garlic**
1/4 cup	**chopped onion**
1/2 cup	**chopped carrots**
1	**ham hock**
1/4 teaspoon	**dried thyme**
5 cups	**chicken broth**
1/2 cup	**heavy whipping cream**
	salt and pepper

Put the beans in a large pot, cover with the water, and bring to a boil over high heat. Boil for 2 minutes and remove from heat. Cover and let the beans soak for 2 hours. Drain the beans well.

In a large heavy saucepan, melt the butter. Add the garlic, onion, and carrots and cook for several minutes until softened. Add the beans, ham hock, thyme, and chicken broth. Bring to a simmer and cook until the beans are tender, about 1 hour.

Remove the ham hock and cool it on a cutting board. Meanwhile, transfer half the soup mixture to a food processor. Purée until smooth and stir back into the soup. Remove the meat from the ham hock, chop it, and stir it into the soup. Slowly stir in the cream and add salt and pepper to taste. Makes 8 servings.

BEAN AND SAUSAGE SOUP

I pound	**bulk Italian pork sausage**
I	**medium onion,** chopped
I	**red bell pepper,** seeded and chopped
I can (15 ounces)	**kidney beans,** rinsed and drained
I can (15 ounces)	**chopped tomatoes**
2 cups	**water**
I	**medium potato,** peeled and cut in $^1/_2$-inch cubes
I	**bay leaf**
I clove	**garlic,** peeled and finely minced
$^1/_2$ teaspoon	**salt**
$^1/_4$ teaspoon	**pepper**
$^1/_4$ teaspoon	**dried thyme**

Brown the sausage in a heavy-bottomed soup pot or Dutch oven over medium heat. Drain sausage on paper towels and reserve I tablespoon drippings. Cook the onion in the reserved drippings for 2 minutes and add the red pepper. Continue cooking until onion and pepper are tender, about 3 minutes. Return the sausage to the pot and add remaining ingredients. Simmer, covered, for I hour. Makes 8 servings.

EASY TACO SOUP

1 pound	**lean ground beef or ground turkey**
1	**medium onion,** diced
1 package (1 ounce)	**taco seasoning**
1 can (15 ounces)	**kidney beans,** rinsed and drained
1 can (15 ounces)	**pinto beans,** rinsed and drained
1 can (15 ounces)	**black beans,** rinsed and drained
1 can (15 ounces)	**diced tomatoes with chiles,** with liquid
1 can (15 ounces)	**corn,** drained
4 cups	**beef broth**
	salt and pepper

Brown the ground beef or turkey in a heavy-bottomed soup pot or Dutch oven over medium heat. Remove the meat with a slotted spoon and drain on paper towels. Pour out all but 1 tablespoon of the pan drippings. Cook the onion in the drippings over medium heat until translucent, about 5 minutes. Return the meat to the pot, add the remaining ingredients, and bring to a simmer. Cook for 20 minutes and season to taste with salt and pepper. Makes 12 servings.

SAVORY CANNELLINI AND KALE STEW

I tablespoon	**olive oil**
I	**onion,** chopped
2 cloves	**garlic,** peeled and minced
I can (28 ounces)	**whole peeled tomatoes**
³/₄ cup	**marinated red peppers,** chopped
I cup	**chicken or vegetable broth**
I can (15 ounces)	**cannellini beans,** drained and rinsed
I bunch	**kale,** washed and chopped
¹/₂ teaspoon	**dried thyme**
	salt and pepper

Heat oil in a large pot over medium heat and cook the onion until translucent, about 5 minutes. Add garlic and cook until fragrant and lightly golden, about 3 minutes. Drain the tomatoes, reserving the juice from the can. Chop the tomatoes, removing any tough core pieces. Add the tomatoes, reserved juice, red peppers, and broth to the pot and stir. Cover and simmer for 20 minutes. Add the beans, kale, and thyme and cook until the kale is tender, about 5 to 6 minutes. Season to taste with salt and pepper. Makes 6 servings.

SLOW COOKER ANASAZI BEAN SOUP

2 cups	**dried anasazi beans or dried beans of your choice,** picked over and rinsed
6 cups	**water**
1 cup	**ham,** cooked and diced
2	**leeks,** white and pale green part only, thinly sliced
2 cloves	**garlic,** peeled and minced
2	**carrots,** scraped and chopped
2 stalks	**celery,** chopped
1 teaspoon	**dried basil**
1 teaspoon	**dried thyme**
1 tablespoon	**Worcestershire sauce**
1 teaspoon	**salt**
1/4 teaspoon	**pepper**
6 cups	**vegetable or chicken broth**

Pour the beans and water in the slow cooker. Cover with the lid but leave the slow cooker off, and soak the beans overnight or for at least 8 hours.

Drain the beans and rinse. Return to the slow cooker and add the remaining ingredients.

Cook on low heat until beans are tender, about 4 to 6 hours. Makes 6 servings.

PASTA E FAGIOLI SOUP

I pound	**ground beef**
I	**onion,** diced
I	**large carrot,** scraped and chopped
3 stalks	**celery,** chopped
2 cloves	**garlic,** peeled and minced
2 cans (15 ounces each)	**diced tomatoes,** with liquid
I can (15 ounces)	**red kidney beans,** rinsed and drained
I can (15 ounces)	**great Northern beans,**
	rinsed and drained
I can (15 ounces)	**tomato sauce**
I can (12 ounces)	**vegetable-tomato juice,** such as V-8
I cup	**chicken stock or broth**
I tablespoon	**white vinegar**
I ½ teaspoons	**salt**
I teaspoon	**oregano**
I teaspoon	**basil**
½ teaspoon	**pepper**
½ teaspoon	**thyme**
½ pound	**ditali or short macaroni pasta**

Brown the ground beef in a large, heavy pot over medium heat. Remove the beef with a slotted spoon and drain on paper towels. Drain off all but I tablespoon of the drippings. Add the onion, carrot, celery, and garlic to the drippings and sauté on medium until vegetables are tender and just starting to brown, 8 to 10 minutes. Add the tomatoes, beans, tomato sauce, vegetable-tomato juice, chicken stock, vinegar, salt, oregano, basil, pepper, and thyme and stir to combine. Increase the heat to medium-high and cook until the mixture starts to simmer. Reduce the heat to medium-low, cover, and simmer for I hour.

Fill a large saucepan with 2 quarts water and heat over high heat to boiling. Add the pasta and cook until it is al dente; drain. Add the pasta to the soup and simmer for 5 minutes. Makes 8 servings.

TAMALE BEAN SOUP

I tablespoon	**olive oil**
I	**onion,** chopped
I	**red bell pepper,** seeded and diced
I can (15 ounces)	**black beans,** rinsed and drained
I can (15 ounces)	**corn,** rinsed and drained
I can (4 ounces)	**diced green chiles**
I can (15 ounces)	**red enchilada sauce**
4 cups	**chicken broth**
½ cup	**polenta**
2 cups	**chopped cooked chicken**
	salt and pepper
I	**ripe avocado,** peeled and diced
¼ cup	**chopped cilantro**
I cup	**grated cheddar cheese**

Heat the oil in a soup pot or large Dutch oven over medium heat and add the onion. Cook for 3 minutes and add the red pepper; cook for an additional 6 to 8 minutes until onion just starts to brown and pepper is tender.

Add the beans, corn, chiles, enchilada sauce, and chicken broth and stir to combine. Add the polenta and use a whisk to incorporate. Turn heat to medium-high and bring the soup to a boil, whisking occasionally. Reduce to a simmer and cook 20 minutes, stirring often. Add the chicken and cook for 10 more minutes; season to taste with salt and pepper. Serve in heated soup bowls topped with diced avocado, cilantro, and cheese. Makes 6 to 8 servings.

LENTIL, SAUSAGE, AND KALE SOUP

I tablespoon	**olive oil**
I pound	**bulk hot sausage**
I	**onion,** chopped
2 stalks	**celery,** chopped, leafy tops reserved
I	**large carrot,** peeled and chopped
I	**large potato,** peeled and cut in ¼-inch cubes
I	**Anaheim pepper,** thinly sliced or finely chopped
2 large cloves	**garlic,** peeled and chopped or sliced
I bunch	**kale,** thinly sliced
6 cups	**chicken stock or broth**
2 cups	**water**
I cup	**dry lentils**
¼ cup	**tomato paste**
I teaspoon	**ground cumin**
	salt and pepper

Heat the oil in a soup pot or large Dutch oven over medium heat and add the sausage, breaking it into pieces. Cook until lightly browned and transfer with a slotted spoon to paper towels to drain. Add the onion, celery, carrot, potato, chile pepper, and garlic to the pan and cook over medium heat until tender, 8 to 10 minutes.

Add the kale and cook for 2 minutes. Add the reserved sausage, stock, water, lentils, tomato paste, and cumin and stir. Increase heat to medium-high and cook until mixture comes to a boil; reduce heat to low and simmer uncovered until the lentils are tender, 30 to 45 minutes. Season to taste with salt and pepper. Makes 6 servings.

NAVY BEAN SOUP

1 pound	**dried navy beans,** rinsed and picked over
6 cups	**chicken broth**
1 can (15 ounces)	**diced tomatoes**
1	**onion,** chopped
2 stalks	**celery,** chopped
3 cloves	**garlic,** peeled and minced
1/2 pound	**chopped ham**
2 tablespoons	**Worcestershire sauce**
1 tablespoon	**dried parsley**
1	**bay leaf**
	salt and pepper

Combine beans, chicken broth, tomatoes, onion, celery, garlic, ham, Worcestershire sauce, parsley, and bay leaf in a stock pot; heat over medium-high until mixture comes to a boil. Lower heat, cover, and simmer for 4 hours or until beans are tender, stirring occasionally and adding water if mixture becomes too thick. Season with salt and pepper and discard bay leaf before serving. Makes 8 servings.

CREAMY CARROT CHICKPEA SOUP

2 tablespoons	**olive oil**
1	**medium onion,** chopped
2 cloves	**garlic,** peeled and minced
1/2 teaspoon	**ground cumin**
1/2 teaspoon	**curry powder**
1/4 teaspoon	**ground ginger**
1 1/2 pounds	**carrots,** scraped and coarsely chopped
1 can (15 ounces)	**garbanzo beans,** rinsed and drained
4 cups	**chicken stock or broth**
1 cup	**water**
1/2 cup	**canned coconut milk**
3/4 teaspoon	**salt**

In a large saucepan, heat olive oil over medium heat. Add onion and garlic and cook about 5 minutes or until tender, stirring occasionally. Stir in cumin, curry powder, and ginger and cook 1 minute. Add the carrots, beans, stock, and water and bring to a boil over medium-high heat.

Reduce heat to medium-low, cover, and simmer until carrots are tender, 20 to 25 minutes. Stir in coconut milk and salt and remove soup from heat.

In a food processor, purée half of the soup in batches until smooth. Return the puréed soup to the pot and heat on medium for 5 minutes or until soup just starts to simmer. Makes 4 servings.

EASY BLACK BEAN SALSA SOUP

2 cans (15 ounces each)	**black beans,** drained and rinsed
1 ½ cups	**chicken broth**
1 cup	**salsa**
1 teaspoon	**ground cumin**
	salt and pepper
4 tablespoons	**sour cream**
2 tablespoons	**thinly sliced green onion**

In a food processor or blender, combine 1 can of beans, broth, salsa, and cumin. Blend until smooth.

In a large saucepan, combine the bean mixture with the remaining can of beans and cook over medium heat, stirring occasionally, until soup starts to simmer. Season to taste with salt and pepper.

Ladle soup into 4 individual bowls and top each bowl with 1 tablespoon of sour cream and ½ tablespoon green onions. Makes 4 servings.

VEGETABLE BEAN SOUP

I tablespoon	**vegetable oil**
I	**onion,** chopped
2 cloves	**garlic,** peeled and minced
2	**carrots,** chopped
I	**medium zucchini,** cut in $^1\!/_2$-inch pieces
3 cups	**vegetable stock or broth**
I can (15 ounces)	**white beans,** rinsed and drained
I can (15 ounces)	**kidney beans,** rinsed and drained
I $^1\!/_2$ cups	**frozen corn kernels,** thawed
I can (14.5 ounces)	**diced tomatoes,** with liquid
$^1\!/_4$ teaspoon	**salt**
$^1\!/_4$ teaspoon	**pepper**

In a large saucepan, heat the oil over medium heat and cook the onion, garlic, carrots, and zucchini, stirring occasionally, for about 5 minutes or until onion is softened. Add the stock, beans, corn, tomatoes, salt, and pepper and continue cooking until soup comes to a boil.

Reduce heat, cover, and simmer for 10 to 15 minutes or until carrots are tender. Makes 6 servings.

RED CHILI

1 pound	**lean ground beef**
1 cup	**chopped onion**
1 clove	**garlic,** peeled and minced
1 can (4 ounces)	**chopped green chiles**
1 can (15 ounces)	**chili beans**
1 can (29 ounces)	**tomato sauce**
1 1/2 cups	**beef broth**
2 tablespoons	**chili powder**
2 teaspoons	**ground cumin**
1 teaspoon	**salt**

In a large skillet, brown the ground beef and onion over medium-high heat for 5 minutes. Add the garlic and green chiles and continue cooking, stirring occasionally, until the onion is translucent and the ground beef is thoroughly cooked. Drain off any fat and add the remaining ingredients. Cook until the mixture bubbles, then reduce the heat to low, cover, and simmer for 30 minutes. Makes 6 servings.

TEX-MEX WHITE CHILI

I tablespoon	**vegetable oil**
I pound	**lean pork tenderloin,** cut in $1/2$-inch cubes
	salt and pepper
$1/2$ cup	**chopped onion**
2 cloves	**garlic,** peeled and minced
$3\,1/2$ cups	**chicken stock or broth**
I can (I5 ounces)	**navy beans, great Northern beans, or white kidney beans,** rinsed and drained
I can (4 ounces)	**diced green chiles**
I tablespoon	**chili powder**
$1/2$ teaspoon	**ground cumin**
$1/2$ cup	**grated Monterey Jack cheese**
I to 2 tablespoons	**snipped fresh cilantro or parsley**

Heat oil in heavy skillet over medium-high heat. Add pork, season with salt and pepper, and cook until browned, stirring frequently, approximately 6 minutes. Remove pork with a slotted spoon and drain on paper towels.

Add onion to the pan and cook over medium heat for 4 to 5 minutes, or until translucent. Add garlic and cook for another 2 minutes, or until lightly browned. Transfer the onion mixture and pork to a large soup pot.

Stir in chicken stock, beans, green chiles, chili powder, and cumin and bring to a boil over medium-high heat. Reduce heat to low, cover, and simmer over low heat until pork is tender, stirring occasionally, approximately I hour.

Ladle into bowls and top with cheese and cilantro or parsley. Makes 6 servings.

TWO-WAY CINCINNATI CHILI

2 pounds	**ground beef**
2	**onions,** chopped
2 cloves	**garlic,** peeled and minced
2 cans (15 ounces each)	**chili beans**
2 cups	**beef stock or broth**
1 can (15 ounces)	**tomato sauce**
1 tablespoon	**Worcestershire sauce**
2 tablespoons	**chili powder**
2 tablespoons	**cocoa**
2 teaspoons	**ground cinnamon**
2 teaspoons	**ground cumin**
1 teaspoon	**salt**
½ teaspoon	**cayenne pepper** (optional)
¼ teaspoon	**ground allspice**
¼ teaspoon	**ground cloves**
1 pound	**linguine**
2 cups	**grated cheddar cheese**

In a large frying pan over medium-high heat, cook the ground beef, stirring occasionally, until browned; drain off fat. Add the onions and garlic and cook until tender. Transfer to a large pot and add the beans, beef stock, tomato sauce, and Worcestershire sauce; stir to combine and heat over medium.

In a small bowl, combine the chili powder, cocoa, cinnamon, cumin, salt, cayenne pepper, allspice, and cloves. Add to the beef mixture and simmer, uncovered, for 1 hour. Adjust seasonings.

Heat a large pot of water to boiling over high heat and cook the linguine until tender; drain. Serve the chili over the hot linguine topped with grated cheese. Makes 8 to 10 servings.

BRUNSWICK STEW

2 quarts	**water**
1 (3 1/2-pound)	**whole chicken,** cut up
2 cans (28 ounces each)	**whole tomatoes,** chopped, with liquid
1 can (15 ounces)	**baby lima beans,** rinsed and drained
1 package (16 ounces)	**frozen baby lima beans**
3	**medium potatoes,** peeled and diced
1	**large onion,** diced
1 can (15 ounces)	**cream-style corn**
1 can (15 ounces)	**corn,** drained
1/4 cup	**sugar**
1/4 cup	**butter**
2 teaspoons	**salt**
1 teaspoon	**pepper**
2 teaspoons	**hot sauce**

Bring water and chicken to a boil in a Dutch oven. Reduce heat and simmer for 40 minutes or until tender. Remove chicken and set aside. Pour out all but 3 1/2 cups broth from Dutch oven, reserving for another use. Add the tomatoes to Dutch oven and bring to a boil over medium-high heat. Cook, stirring often, for 40 minutes or until liquid is reduced by about a third.

Skin, bone, and shred the chicken. In a small bowl, mash the canned lima beans with a potato masher to the consistency of mashed potatoes. Add the chicken, mashed beans, frozen lima beans, potatoes, and onion to the pot. Cook over low heat, stirring often, for 3 1/2 hours. Stir in the remaining ingredients and cook over low heat, stirring often, for 1 hour. Adjust seasonings if needed. Makes 8 to 10 servings.

CLASSIC MINESTRONE

¹/₄ pound	**bacon,** diced
4 cloves	**garlic,** peeled and minced
2	**carrots,** peeled and cut in ¹/₄-inch dice
1	**onion,** peeled and cut in ¹/₄-inch dice
1	**leek** (white part and 1 inch of green part), rinsed and cut in ¹/₄-inch dice
3 cups	**finely shredded green cabbage**
1	**small zucchini,** cut in ¹/₄-inch dice
1	**potato,** peeled and cut in ¹/₄-inch dice
4 cups	**chicken stock or broth**
2 cups	**beef stock or broth**
2 tablespoons	**tomato paste**
5 tablespoons	**chopped flat-leaf parsley,** divided
2 teaspoons	**dried oregano**
1 ¹/₂ teaspoons	**dried basil**
1 teaspoon	**black pepper**
	salt, to taste
1 can (15 ounces)	**cannellini beans,** rinsed and drained
1 can (15 ounces)	**kidney beans,** rinsed and drained
4 ripe	**plum tomatoes,** cut in ¹/₄-inch dice
¹/₂ cup	**small pasta** (tiny shells or bow shapes)
	freshly grated Parmesan cheese

Cook the bacon in a large, heavy pot over medium heat until it barely starts to brown, about 5 minutes. Spoon onto paper towels to drain. Add the garlic, carrots, onion, and leek to the drippings and cook, stirring occasionally, until tender, 8 to 10 minutes. Add the cabbage, zucchini, potato, stocks, and tomato paste. Bring to a boil. Reduce the heat and add 2 tablespoons of the parsley, the oregano, basil, pepper, and salt. Simmer over medium heat for 15 minutes. Add the beans, tomatoes, and pasta; stir and simmer until the pasta is tender, about 10 minutes. Adjust the seasonings. Stir in the remaining 3 tablespoons parsley just before serving. Garnish each bowl with Parmesan cheese. Makes 6 to 8 servings.

DINNERS

CANNELLINI BEANS WITH SMOKED SAUSAGE AND GARLIC

1 tablespoon	**olive oil**
2 pounds	**kielbasa sausage,** cut in ½-inch slices
1 can (15 ounces)	**cannellini beans,** rinsed and drained
1 cup	**chicken broth**
2 cloves	**garlic,** peeled and chopped
8	**cherry tomatoes,** quartered
1 bunch	**parsley,** chopped, divided
	salt and pepper

Heat the oil in a heavy pot over medium-high heat and add the
sausage. Cook until lightly browned, about 5 minutes. Add the beans,
broth, garlic, tomatoes, and half the parsley and stir to combine.
Reduce heat and simmer for 30 minutes. Season to taste with salt
and pepper. Sprinkle with remaining parsley before serving. Makes
6 servings.

PINTO BEANS, BACON, AND RICE

3 slices	**bacon,** cut in half
I	**small onion,** chopped
¼ cup	**ketchup**
2 tablespoons	**brown sugar**
I teaspoon	**Dijon mustard**
½ teaspoon	**salt**
¼ teaspoon	**pepper**
I ½ cups	**cooked rice**
I can (15 ounces)	**pinto beans,** rinsed and drained

Preheat oven to 350 degrees and grease a 2-quart casserole dish.

In a large skillet over medium heat, partially cook the bacon until it just begins to brown. Remove bacon from skillet, drain on a paper towel, and pour out all but I tablespoon of the grease from the pan. Add the onion to the skillet and cook until translucent. Add the ketchup, brown sugar, mustard, salt, and pepper and stir until combined. Add rice and beans and stir.

Transfer mixture to prepared casserole dish and arrange the bacon strips on top. Bake uncovered for about 30 minutes, or until bacon is crispy and casserole is hot and bubbly. Makes 4 servings.

TACO CASSEROLE

2 tablespoons	**vegetable oil**
¾ cup	**chopped onion**
I pound	**ground beef or ground turkey**
2 cloves	**garlic,** peeled and minced
I tablespoon	**chili powder**
2 teaspoons	**ground cumin**
2 teaspoons	**ground coriander**
	salt and pepper, to taste
I can (8 ounces)	**tomato sauce**
2 cups	**coarsely crushed corn chips**
2 cups	**grated Mexican blend or cheddar cheese,** divided
I can (15 ounces)	**refried beans,** heated through
I cup	**salsa**
2	**green onions,** chopped
I can (2.25 ounces)	**sliced black olives,** drained
	lettuce and tomato, for serving

Preheat oven to 375 degrees and grease an 8 x 8-inch baking dish. Heat the oil in a large skillet over medium heat; add the onion and cook, stirring often, until softened, about 4 to 5 minutes. Add the beef and cook, stirring to break up, until cooked through, about 5 minutes. Drain off the grease and add the garlic and spices. Cook over medium heat for 30 seconds and add the tomato sauce. Turn the heat to low and simmer for about 10 minutes, stirring occasionally. Remove from heat and cover.

Spread the corn chips evenly in the bottom of the baking dish. Add I cup of the cheese to the hot refried beans, stirring until it melts. Add the salsa and stir until combined. Spoon the bean mixture evenly over the chips and top with the meat mixture. Sprinkle the green onions and olives over the meat and sprinkle the remaining cheese evenly on top. Bake for 15 to 20 minutes, or until casserole is bubbly and cheese is melted. Let cool for 5 minutes. Serve sprinkled with lettuce and tomato. Makes 4 servings.

POLYNESIAN BEAN BAKE

1 pound	**lean bacon**
1	**large onion,** chopped
1	**medium green bell pepper,** chopped
1/4 cup	**dark brown sugar**
1/4 cup	**apple cider vinegar**
1/4 cup	**molasses**
1/2 cup	**ketchup**
2 tablespoons	**yellow mustard**
2 cloves	**garlic,** peeled and minced
1 can (15 ounces)	**baked beans**
1 can (15 ounces)	**kidney beans,** rinsed and drained
1 can (15 ounces)	**lima beans,** rinsed and drained
1 can (15 ounces)	**pineapple chunks in juice**

Preheat the oven to 350 degrees and grease a 2-quart casserole dish.

In a large skillet, cook the bacon over medium heat until crispy. Remove bacon, drain on paper towels, and crumble when cool. Pour out all but 2 tablespoons pan drippings and heat over medium heat. Add the onion and cook for 4 minutes. Add the bell pepper and continue cooking until onion is translucent and pepper is tender, about 4 more minutes. Remove from the heat, cover, and reserve.

In a small bowl, combine the brown sugar, vinegar, molasses, ketchup, mustard, and garlic; mix well.

In a large bowl, combine the bacon, onion mixture, baked beans, kidney beans, lima beans, and pineapple with juice. Add the brown sugar mixture and stir to combine. Bake for 1 hour or until bubbling and hot. Makes 8 servings.

BEEF ENCHILADA CASSEROLE

I pound	**lean ground beef**
1/2 teaspoon	**garlic salt**
1/2 teaspoon	**onion powder**
I can (15 ounces)	**refried beans**
I can (10 ounces)	**red enchilada sauce,** divided
12 (6-inch)	**corn tortillas**
2 cups	**grated cheddar cheese**

Preheat oven to 375 degrees and grease a 3-quart casserole dish.

In a large skillet, cook the ground beef with garlic salt and onion powder until lightly browned; drain fat. Add the refried beans and 1/2 cup of the enchilada sauce to the meat and stir to combine.

Pour the remaining enchilada sauce in a shallow dish. Dip 3 tortillas in the sauce and layer on the bottom of the baking dish. Spoon half of the meat mixture on top. Dip 3 more tortillas in the sauce and layer on top of the meat. Sprinkle with half of the cheese. Cover with another layer of 3 tortillas dipped in enchilada sauce. Spoon in remaining meat mixture and top with the remaining 3 tortillas dipped in enchilada sauce. Pour any remaining sauce over the layers and top with remaining cheese.

Cover and bake for 20 minutes. Remove from oven, uncover, and return to oven for 5 minutes or until casserole is hot and bubbly and cheese is melted. Makes 6 servings.

CREOLE RED BEANS AND RICE

4 slices	**bacon**
1/2 pound	**andouille sausage,** cut in 1/2-inch slices
1 cup	**chopped ham**
2	**onions,** chopped
1	**green bell pepper,** seeded and chopped
4 stalks	**celery,** chopped
2 cloves	**garlic,** peeled and minced
1	**bay leaf**
1 teaspoon	**dried thyme**
1/2 teaspoon	**salt**
1/2 teaspoon	**pepper**
4 cups	**chicken broth**
2 cans (15 ounces each)	**kidney beans,** rinsed and drained
3	**Roma tomatoes,** chopped
1 tablespoon	**red wine or balsamic vinegar**
1 teaspoon	**hot pepper sauce**
1 smoked	**ham hock**
4 cups	**hot, cooked white rice**

In a large, heavy pot, cook the bacon over medium-high heat until it just starts to brown. Add the sausage and ham and continue cooking, stirring, until sausage is browned. Add the onions, pepper, celery, garlic, bay leaf, thyme, salt, and pepper and continue cooking, stirring occasionally, until vegetables are tender. Add the broth, beans, tomatoes, vinegar, hot sauce, and ham hock. Continue cooking and stirring for 5 minutes. Increase the heat to high and bring the mixture to a boil. Reduce heat to medium-low and simmer, uncovered, for 1 1/2 hours, adding water if the mixture gets too thick.

Remove the ham hock and let it cool. Transfer 1/4 of the bean mixture to a food processor; purée until smooth and return to the pot. Chop the meat from the ham hock and add it to the pot; heat for 3 more minutes. Divide the rice among 6 plates and top with the beans. Makes 6 servings.

EASY FALAFEL

3/4 cup	**plain Greek yogurt**
1/2 cup	**peeled, chopped cucumber**
1 teaspoon	**dried dill weed**
1 teaspoon	**salt,** divided
1/2 teaspoon	**pepper,** divided
1 can (15 ounces)	**garbanzo beans,** rinsed and drained
1/4 cup	**finely minced onion**
1/2 cup	**fresh parsley**
1/2 teaspoon	**garlic powder**
1	**egg**
2 teaspoons	**ground cumin**
1 teaspoon	**ground coriander**
1 teaspoon	**lemon juice**
1 teaspoon	**baking powder**
1 tablespoon	**olive oil**
1 cup	**dry bread crumbs**
	vegetable oil for frying
2	**fresh pita breads,** halved horizontally
1/2 cup	**chopped romaine lettuce**
1	**ripe tomato,** chopped

In a small bowl, stir together the yogurt, cucumber, dill, 1/2 teaspoon salt, and 1/4 teaspoon pepper until well blended. Cover and chill.

In a large bowl, mash the beans with a potato masher until creamy. Add the onion, parsley, and garlic powder and stir until blended. In a small bowl, combine the egg, cumin, coriander, remaining salt, remaining pepper, lemon juice, and baking powder. Stir into bean mixture. Add the olive oil and stir until blended. Add the bread crumbs a little at a time until the mixture holds together. Divide the mixture and shape in 8 (1/2-inch) patties. Heat 1 inch of oil in a large skillet over medium-high heat. Fry until brown on both sides. Arrange 2 falafel in each pita half with lettuce, chopped tomato, and cucumber sauce. Makes 4 servings.

PORK CHOP 'N' BEAN BAKE

I tablespoon	**vegetable oil**
8	**boneless or bone-in pork chops,** ¹/₂ inch thick
	salt and pepper
	garlic powder
3 cans (15 ounces each)	**pork and beans**
I	**onion,** chopped
I	**green bell pepper,** chopped
³/₄ cup	**ketchup**
¹/₄ cup	**barbecue sauce**
¹/₄ cup	**brown sugar**
I tablespoon	**yellow mustard**
¹/₈ teaspoon	**cayenne pepper**

Preheat oven to 350 degrees and grease a Dutch oven or large casserole dish.

Heat the oil in a large skillet and brown the chops on both sides, in batches if necessary. Season with salt, pepper, and garlic powder to taste; drain and reserve.

In a large bowl, mix together the pork and beans, onion, bell pepper, ketchup, barbecue sauce, brown sugar, mustard, and cayenne. Pour half of the bean mixture in the Dutch oven and arrange the pork chops on top. Top with remaining bean mixture.

Bake, covered, for 45 minutes. Uncover and continue baking for 30 more minutes, or until chops are tender. Makes 8 servings.

GRANDMA'S HAM AND BEANS

1 pound	**dried great Northern beans,** rinsed and picked over
4 cups	**vegetable or chicken broth**
3 cups	**water**
1/2 pound	**cooked ham,** diced
1	**small onion,** diced
1/2 cup	**brown sugar**
1 teaspoon	**salt**
1/2 teaspoon	**pepper**
1/4 teaspoon	**cayenne pepper**
1 tablespoon	**dried parsley**

In a large pot or Dutch oven, cover the beans with cold water and let stand at least 8 hours or overnight. Drain beans in a strainer and rinse.

Return beans to the pot and add the broth, water, ham, onion, brown sugar, salt, pepper, cayenne, and parsley. Stir and cook over medium-high heat until mixture almost reaches a boil; reduce heat to low and simmer uncovered for 1 1/2 to 2 hours, or until beans are tender, adding more water if necessary during cooking time. Makes 8 servings.

MEHICAN CHILAQUILES CASSEROLE

1 tablespoon	**olive oil**
1	**onion,** chopped
1	**tomato,** chopped
1 ½ cups	**fresh or frozen corn**
1 can (15 ounces)	**black beans,** rinsed and drained
2 tablespoons	**lime juice**
1 teaspoon	**salt**
½ teaspoon	**pepper**
2 cups	**baby spinach leaves**
2 cups	**crushed corn tortilla chips**
8 ounces	**grated sharp cheddar cheese**
2 cups	**salsa**

Preheat the oven to 350 degrees and grease an 8 x 8-inch baking pan or casserole dish. Heat the olive oil in a large skillet over medium heat and sauté the onion until translucent, about 6 minutes. Stir in the tomato, corn, black beans, lime juice, salt, and pepper and continue to sauté for another 5 to 10 minutes, until just heated through.

Fill a medium saucepan with water and bring to a boil. Add the spinach and cook just until wilted but still green, about 1 minute. Drain.

Arrange half of the chips in the bottom of the prepared baking dish. Spoon the bean mixture on top and sprinkle with two-thirds of the grated cheese. Spread the spinach evenly over the cheese and drizzle with half of the salsa. Arrange remaining chips on top and cover with the remaining salsa and cheese. Bake, uncovered, until casserole is hot and bubbly and cheese is melted, about 35 to 40 minutes. Makes 4 to 6 servings.

NOTE: For an authentic touch, cut 8 corn tortillas in ½-inch strips, fry in vegetable oil until crispy, and use instead of crushed chips.

PASTA WITH WHITE BEANS AND ARTICHOKE HEARTS

1 pound	**fettuccine**
2 tablespoons	**olive oil,** divided
2 cans (15 ounces each)	**cannellini beans,** drained and rinsed, divided
1/2 cup	**chicken broth**
2 cloves	**garlic,** peeled and minced
1 can (14 ounces)	**artichoke hearts,** drained and chopped
1 teaspoon	**salt**
1/2 teaspoon	**black pepper**
1/3 cup	**half-and-half**
1/2 cup	**grated Parmesan cheese**
2 tablespoons	**chopped flat-leaf parsley**

Cook the fettuccine in boiling water according to the package directions. Drain the pasta and return it to the pot; add 1 tablespoon olive oil and stir with a fork to coat the noodles. Cover and reserve.

In the bowl of a food processor, combine 1 can of the beans and the chicken broth. Process until smooth and creamy; scrape down sides and process again. Reserve.

Meanwhile, heat the remaining 1 tablespoon olive oil in a large skillet over medium heat. Add the garlic and cook, stirring, for 1 minute. Add the bean mixture, the remaining drained beans, artichoke hearts, salt, and pepper. Cook until heated through, 3 to 4 minutes. Add the half-and-half and continue cooking, stirring frequently, until heated through, about 4 minutes. (If sauce is too thick, add additional half-and-half.) Correct seasonings if needed. Divide the pasta among 6 heated plates and top with the sauce. Sprinkle with Parmesan cheese and chopped parsley. Makes 6 servings.

CRISPY BEAN FLAUTAS WITH GUACAMOLE

I can (15 ounces)	**refried beans**
½ cup	**cream cheese,** softened
½ cup	**salsa,** divided
I teaspoon	**chili powder**
½ teaspoon	**cumin**
2	**green onions,** chopped
⅔ cup	**grated Mexican cheese blend**
12 (6-inch)	**flour tortillas**
⅓ cup	**vegetable oil**
	salt for sprinkling
2	**large, ripe avocados,** halved, pitted and flesh removed

Preheat the oven to 425 degrees and line a baking sheet with foil or parchment paper.

In a large bowl, combine the refried beans, cream cheese, ¼ cup of the salsa, chili powder, cumin, green onions, and cheese; stir until well blended. Lay a tortilla on a work surface and spoon about 2 tablespoons of the bean mixture along the middle. Roll the tortilla tightly around the filling and secure with a toothpick. Repeat with remaining tortillas and filling and arrange flautas on prepared baking sheet.

Brush the tops lightly with oil and sprinkle them with salt. Bake for 15 to 20 minutes, until crisp and browned. While flautas are cooking, combine the avocado and remaining ¼ cup salsa in a small bowl and use a fork to gently smash the avocado, making guacamole.

Remove the flautas from the oven and cool for 5 minutes before removing toothpicks. Serve accompanied with guacamole. Makes 6 servings.

GARLICKY WHITE BEANS AND SHRIMP

4 tablespoons	**olive oil,** divided
I pound	**medium raw shrimp,** peeled and deveined
I teaspoon	**paprika**
3 cloves	**garlic,** peeled and minced, divided
½ teaspoon	**red pepper flakes**
I	**bay leaf**
I can (14.5 ounces)	**diced tomatoes,** with liquid
I tablespoon	**tomato paste**
2 cans (15 ounces each)	**cannellini beans,** rinsed and drained
2 tablespoons	**chopped flat-leaf parsley**

Heat I tablespoon olive oil in a large skillet over medium-high heat until it shimmers. Add the shrimp and sauté for I minute. Sprinkle with the paprika and add half of the garlic to the pan. Stir and continue cooking for I to 2 minutes, or until shrimp is pink and opaque. Transfer the shrimp to a bowl and set aside.

Add 2 tablespoons olive oil to the pan and add the remaining garlic, pepper flakes, and bay leaf. Cook until garlic is golden brown, I to 2 minutes. Add the tomatoes and their juice, and cook until most of the liquid evaporates, about 4 minutes. Add the tomato paste and continue cooking for 2 more minutes. Add the beans and cook until heated through, about 5 minutes. Stir in the shrimp and cook just until heated through, about 2 minutes. Drizzle with remaining I tablespoon olive oil and sprinkle with parsley. Makes 4 servings.

ORIENTAL BEEF
WITH STRING BEANS

1/4 cup	**cornstarch**
1/2 cup	**soy sauce**
2 tablespoons	**water**
4 teaspoons	**peeled and minced fresh gingerroot**
2 cloves	**garlic,** peeled and minced
4 tablespoons	**vegetable oil,** divided
I pound	**boneless beef sirloin steak,** cut in 1/4-inch strips
I pound	**fresh green beans,** ends trimmed
I teaspoon	**sugar**
1/2 teaspoon	**salt**
	hot, cooked rice

In a bowl, combine the cornstarch, soy sauce, water, ginger, garlic, and 2 tablespoons of the oil until smooth. Pour the marinade in a large shallow dish. Add the beef to the dish, stir with a fork to coat with marinade, and refrigerate for 30 minutes.

Drain the beef, reserving the marinade. In a wok or large skillet, heat the remaining oil over medium-high heat until it just shimmers and fry the beef, stirring constantly, for 4 to 6 minutes or until done. Using a slotted spoon, remove the beef to a bowl and cover with foil to keep warm. Add the beans, sugar, and salt to the pan and cook until beans are tender, about 8 to 10 minutes. Stir in the beef and reserved marinade. Cook, stirring constantly, until mixture comes to a boil and thickens slightly. Serve over hot rice. Makes 6 servings.

GARBANZO BURGERS

1 can (15 ounces)	**garbanzo beans,** rinsed and drained
3 tablespoons	**water**
1 teaspoon	**lemon juice**
1 cup	**dry bread crumbs**
1	**egg,** lightly beaten
1/2 teaspoon	**garlic powder**
1/2 teaspoon	**onion powder**
1/2 teaspoon	**salt**
1/4 teaspoon	**pepper**
2 tablespoons	**vegetable oil**
6	**hamburger buns,** split and toasted
6 slices	**cheese**
6 leaves	**lettuce**
	pickle slices, mayonnaise,
	ketchup, and mustard

Place the beans, water, and lemon juice in a food processor; cover and process until blended. Scrape down the sides and process again. Transfer the mixture to a large bowl and add the bread crumbs, egg, garlic powder, onion powder, salt, and pepper; stir until combined. Shape the mixture into six 1/2-inch-thick patties; reserve.

Heat the oil in a large skillet over medium-high heat and cook the patties until lightly browned, about 3 to 4 minutes. Flip the patties and continue cooking until lightly browned. Transfer the patties to buns and top with cheese slices and lettuce. Serve with pickle slices, mayonnaise, ketchup, and mustard. Makes 6 servings.

CLASSIC CASSOULET

³/₄ pound	**dried navy beans,** sorted and rinsed
I	**bay leaf**
4 cups	**chicken broth**
¹/₄ pound	**bacon,** diced
4	**boneless chicken thighs**
2	**medium carrots,** cut in I-inch slices
2	**medium onions,** quartered
I can (8 ounces)	**diced tomatoes,** with liquid
I large stalk	**celery with leaves,** coarsely chopped
2 cloves	**garlic,** crushed
I teaspoon	**salt**
¹/₂ teaspoon	**dried marjoram**
¹/₄ teaspoon	**pepper**
¹/₂ pound	**smoked sausage,** cut in 2-inch slices
	chopped fresh parsley

In a large soup pot, combine the beans, 3 cups water, and bay leaf. Bring to a boil and cook, uncovered, for 2 minutes. Remove from the heat; cover and let stand for 4 hours. Drain and rinse the beans and return to pot. Stir in broth and bring the mixture to a boil. Reduce heat to medium-low, cover, and simmer until beans are tender, about I hour.

Cook the bacon in a skillet over medium heat until crisp. Drain on paper towels and crumble. Pour out all but 2 tablespoons of the pan drippings and cook the chicken over medium heat until browned on all sides.

Preheat the oven to 350 degrees. In a 3-quart baking dish, combine the beans with cooking liquid, bacon, carrots, onions, tomatoes, celery, garlic, salt, marjoram, pepper, and sausage. Arrange the chicken pieces on top. Cover and bake for 30 minutes. Remove from oven and add additional water if beans appear dry. Cover and continue cooking for 60 minutes. Discard bay leaf and garnish with parsley. Makes 6 servings.

MACARONI A LA MINESTRONE

1 pound	**ground beef**
2 cans (14.5 ounces each)	**Italian diced tomatoes,** with liquid
2¼ cups	**water**
1½ cups	**uncooked elbow macaroni**
2 teaspoons	**beef bouillon granules**
1 can (15 ounces)	**kidney beans,** rinsed and drained
1 can (15 ounces)	**garbanzo beans or chickpeas,** rinsed and drained
1 can (15 ounces)	**cut green beans,** rinsed and drained
	salt and pepper
	grated Parmesan cheese

In a large skillet, cook beef over medium heat until no longer pink; drain. Add the tomatoes, water, macaroni, and bouillon; bring to a boil.

Reduce heat; cover and simmer for about 15 minutes, or until macaroni is tender. Stir in all beans and cook until heated through. Season with salt and pepper to taste. Serve accompanied with grated Parmesan cheese. Makes 6 servings.

CHEESY MEXICAN RICE AND BEANS SKILLET

1 tablespoon	**olive oil**
2 cloves	**garlic,** peeled and minced
1	**small onion,** diced
1	**small green or red bell pepper,** diced
3 cups	**cooked rice**
1 can (15 ounces)	**black beans,** rinsed and drained
1 can (15 ounces)	**corn,** drained
1 can (10 ounces)	**mild green enchilada sauce**
1 teaspoon	**chili powder**
1/2 teaspoon	**cumin**
1/4 teaspoon	**dried oregano**
	salt and pepper
1 cup	**grated Mexican blend cheese**
2 tablespoons	**chopped fresh cilantro**

Heat olive oil in a large skillet over medium-high heat. Add garlic, onion, and bell pepper and cook, stirring frequently, until onion is translucent, about 4 minutes. Add the rice, black beans, corn, enchilada sauce, chili powder, cumin, and oregano and cook, stirring, until well combined and heated through, about 3 to 4 minutes; season to taste with salt and pepper. Remove from heat and top with cheese. Cover until cheese has melted, about 2 minutes. Serve garnished with cilantro. Makes 4 servings.

SIDE DISHES

BUTTER BEANS WITH BACON AND CARAMELIZED ONIONS

4 slices	**thick bacon,** diced
2	**onions,** divided
2 stalks	**celery,** diced
2 cloves	**garlic,** peeled and minced
2 cans (15 ounces each)	**butter beans,** rinsed and drained
	salt and pepper
³/₄ teaspoon	**chopped fresh thyme leaves**

In a medium skillet over medium heat, cook the bacon until lightly browned, 8 to 10 minutes. Remove with a slotted spoon and drain on paper towels. Pour off 2 tablespoons of the drippings from the pan and reserve.

Chop 1 onion and add it to the remaining drippings in the skillet along with the celery and garlic. Cook, stirring frequently, until tender, about 10 minutes. Add the beans to the pan and stir. Season to taste with salt and pepper, reduce heat to low, cover, and simmer.

In another medium skillet, heat the reserved bacon drippings over medium-low heat. Slice the remaining onion and add it to the pan. Sprinkle with about ¹/₂ teaspoon salt and cook, stirring, until onions are transparent, about 5 minutes. Reduce heat to low and cook, stirring occasionally, until the onions become browned and caramelized, 30 to 45 minutes. Add 2 tablespoons water and stir to loosen any browned bits on the bottom of the pan. Add the bacon to the caramelized onions and heat gently.

To serve, divide the bean mixture among 4 plates and top each with some of the caramelized onion mixture. Garnish with the chopped thyme. Makes 4 servings.

RANCH GREEN BEANS

1/4 cup	**bread crumbs**
1/4 teaspoon	**salt**
1 pound	**fresh green beans,** ends trimmed
2 tablespoons	**butter**
1/2 pound	**mushrooms,** sliced
1	**medium onion,** chopped
2 cloves	**garlic,** peeled and minced
2 tablespoons	**flour**
1 1/2 cups	**milk,** divided
2 tablespoons	**ranch salad dressing mix**
1/4 teaspoon	**pepper**

Heat the oven to 350 degrees and spread the bread crumbs on a baking sheet. Bake just until lightly browned, about 4 to 5 minutes. Sprinkle with salt and set pan on a wire rack to cool; reserve.

Put the beans in a large pot, cover with water and bring to a boil over high heat. Cook until tender, about 5 minutes. Drain and reserve.

Meanwhile, in a large skillet, heat butter over medium-high heat. Add the mushrooms and onion and cook, stirring, until lightly browned, about 5 minutes. Add the garlic and cook, stirring, for 1 minute longer.

In a small bowl, whisk together the flour and 2 tablespoons milk until smooth. Whisk in the remaining milk and stir into mushroom mixture. Cook, stirring constantly, until mixture comes to a boil. Add salad dressing mix and pepper and continue cooking, stirring constantly, for 2 minutes. Add the beans and cook until heated through, 3 to 4 minutes. Transfer to a serving dish and sprinkle with reserved bread crumbs. Makes 6 servings.

PORK LOVERS'
MAPLE BAKED BEANS

2 cups	**dried navy beans**
1/2 cup	**maple syrup**
1 teaspoon	**dry mustard**
1 teaspoon	**salt**
6 strips	**bacon,** chopped
1 smoked	**ham hock**
1	**onion,** chopped
2 tablespoons	**butter**
2 tablespoons	**dark brown sugar**

Put the beans in a large pot, cover with water, and bring to a boil over high heat. Boil for 30 minutes. Drain beans and discard cooking liquid.

Preheat oven to 325 degrees. In a medium bowl, combine 2 cups water, maple syrup, mustard, and salt. Put the chopped bacon at the bottom of a Dutch oven. Spoon half of the beans and half of the onion on top of the bacon. Add the ham hock, followed by the remaining beans and onion. Pour the maple syrup mixture evenly over the beans and cover with a lid. Bake for 3 hours, or until beans are tender and the meat from the ham hock is pulling away from the bone. Add more water if necessary during cooking.

Remove the pot from the oven and use a slotted spoon to remove the ham hock; transfer it to a cutting board and cool. Remove the meat, chop it, and stir it into the beans.

In a small bowl, combine the butter and brown sugar. Dot the beans with the mixture and return to the oven, uncovered; bake for an additional 30 minutes. Makes 8 servings.

FIVE TIMES BETTER BAKED BEANS

6 slices	**bacon**
1 cup	**chopped onion**
1 clove	**garlic,** peeled and minced
1 can (15 ounces)	**pinto beans,** rinsed and drained
1 can (15 ounces)	**great Northern beans,** rinsed and drained
1 can (15 ounces)	**baked beans**
1 can (15 ounces)	**kidney beans,** rinsed and drained
1 can (15 ounces)	**garbanzo beans,** rinsed and drained
³/₄ cup	**ketchup**
¹/₂ cup	**molasses**
¹/₄ cup	**packed brown sugar**
2 tablespoons	**Worcestershire sauce**
1 tablespoon	**yellow mustard**
¹/₂ teaspoon	**pepper**

Preheat oven to 375 degrees and grease a 9 x 12-inch baking dish.

Cook bacon in a large skillet over medium-high heat, turning occasionally until evenly brown. Drain, reserving 2 tablespoons of drippings, and reserve. Cook the onion and garlic in the reserved drippings until onion is tender, about 5 minutes. Drain excess grease and transfer mixture to a large mixing bowl.

Add the pinto beans, great Northern beans, baked beans, kidney beans, and garbanzo beans. Stir in the ketchup, molasses, brown sugar, Worcestershire sauce, mustard, and pepper; crumble and add the bacon. Mix well and transfer to the prepared baking dish. Cover and bake for 1 hour. Makes 12 to 18 servings.

COLA BEANS

$\frac{1}{2}$ pound	**bacon,** strips cut in half widthwise
4 cans (28 ounces each)	**baked beans,** drained
I cup	**dark brown sugar**
I can (12 ounces)	**cola**

Preheat the oven to 350 degrees and grease a large baking dish.

In a large skillet over medium heat, cook the bacon until partially done and just starting to brown. Drain the bacon strips on paper towels.

Spoon one can of the baked beans in the prepared dish and top with $\frac{1}{4}$ of the bacon strips. Sprinkle evenly with $\frac{1}{4}$ cup brown sugar. Repeat with the remaining beans, bacon, and brown sugar. Pour the can of cola over the top and cover. Bake for I hour. Makes 12 servings.

GREEN BEANS, BABY POTATOES, AND BACON

6 slices	**bacon,** chopped
3 tablespoons	**butter**
1	**red onion,** chopped
2 pounds	**fresh green beans,** ends trimmed
8	**small new potatoes,** cut in $1/4$ x $1/4$-inch dice
1 large clove	**garlic,** peeled and minced
$1/4$ cup	**chicken broth**
$1 1/2$ teaspoons	**balsamic vinegar**
	salt and pepper

Cook the bacon in a large skillet over medium heat, stirring occasionally, until evenly browned, 8 to 10 minutes. Transfer the bacon to paper towels and drain.

Drain the grease, wipe out the skillet, and heat the butter over medium heat until it melts. Add the onion and cook until translucent, about 5 minutes. Increase the heat to medium-high and add the cooked bacon, green beans, potatoes, garlic, and chicken broth. Bring to a boil, cover, and simmer over low heat until the green beans are tender, about 10 minutes. Sprinkle with vinegar and season to taste with salt and pepper. Makes 8 servings.

EASY SUMMER SUCCOTASH

I cup	**butter,** divided
2 cups	**fresh lima beans**
¹/₂ teaspoon	**salt**
4	**fresh tomatoes,** peeled and chopped
2 teaspoons	**sugar**
4 ears	**fresh corn kernels,** cut from the cob
	salt and pepper

Melt ¹/₂ cup butter in a large saucepan over medium heat. Stir in the lima beans and salt and cook until tender, about 20 minutes.

Meanwhile, melt the remaining ¹/₂ cup butter in a medium saucepan over medium heat and add the tomatoes and sugar. Cook until the tomatoes are tender and mixture thickens slightly, about 20 minutes.

Stir the tomato mixture into the lima bean mixture and add the corn kernels. Continue cooking, stirring occasionally, until corn is tender, 6 to 8 minutes. Season to taste with salt and pepper. Makes 6 servings.

THREE GRACES
VEGETABLE MEDLEY

I pound	**fresh green beans,** cut in I-inch pieces
4	**medium carrots,** cut in 2-inch x ¼-inch pieces
4 tablespoons	**butter**
I	**onion,** sliced
I pound	**fresh mushrooms,** sliced
I teaspoon	**salt**
½ teaspoon	**pepper**
¼ teaspoon	**garlic salt**

Bring a large pot of water over high heat until it boils. Add the green beans and carrots and cook until tender but still firm, about 5 minutes. Drain.

Melt the butter in a large skillet over medium heat. Cook the onion until transparent, about 4 minutes. Add the mushrooms and cook until the mushrooms are tender and the onion is lightly browned. Add the green beans, carrots, salt, pepper, and garlic salt. Cover and cook for 5 minutes. Makes 8 servings.

LUCKY BLACK-EYED PEAS

6 slices	**bacon**
1	**large onion,** chopped
1 stalk	**celery,** diced
4 cloves	**garlic,** peeled and minced
6 cups	**chicken broth**
$1/2$ teaspoon	**salt**
$1/4$ teaspoon	**pepper**
4 cups	**fresh or frozen black-eyed peas**

In a large pot or Dutch oven, cook bacon over medium heat until crisp; drain on paper towels and pour out all but 2 tablespoons of the drippings.

Cook the onion, celery, and garlic in the drippings over medium heat until tender, about 5 minutes. Add the broth, salt, pepper, and black-eyed peas. Increase the heat to medium-high and bring to a boil. Crumble and add the bacon. Lower the heat, cover, and simmer until peas are tender, about 1 hour. Makes 6 to 8 servings.

GLAZED SWEET POTATOES AND GARBANZOS

2 tablespoons	**lime juice**
2 tablespoons	**butter,** melted
2 tablespoons	**honey**
1 tablespoon	**olive oil**
1 clove	**garlic,** peeled and minced
1 teaspoon	**dried ginger**
1 teaspoon	**salt**
1/2 teaspoon	**pepper**
3	**large sweet potatoes** (about 3 pounds), peeled and cut in 1/2-inch cubes
2 cans (15 ounces each)	**garbanzo beans,** rinsed and drained
1	**onion,** finely chopped
1 tablespoon	**chopped fresh thyme leaves**

Preheat the oven to 425 degrees and grease a rimmed baking sheet.

In a large bowl, whisk together the lime juice, melted butter, honey, oil, garlic, ginger, salt, and pepper. Add the sweet potatoes, garbanzo beans, onion, and thyme and stir.

Spread the mixture evenly in the prepared baking sheet. Bake for 35 to 40 minutes, stirring once about halfway through cooking time. Cool for 5 minutes before serving. Makes 6 servings.

MILLIONAIRE BEANS

¹/₂ cup	**blanched slivered almonds**
¹/₂ teaspoon	**salt**
1 tablespoon	**fresh lemon juice**
1¹/₂ pounds	**fresh green beans,** ends trimmed
2 slices	**bacon**
1	**small onion,** chopped
2 tablespoons	**teriyaki sauce**
1 tablespoon	**honey**

Heat the oven to 350 degrees and spread the almonds evenly in a single layer on an ungreased baking sheet. Bake for 5 minutes; remove from the oven and stir. Bake for an additional 3 to 5 minutes, or until lightly toasted. Sprinkle with salt and cool.

Bring a large pot of water to a boil and add the lemon juice. Add the beans and cook until crisp-tender, about 5 minutes. Drain in a colander and run cold water over the beans to stop cooking. Drain well and reserve.

In a skillet, cook the bacon until very crispy. Remove bacon from pan, cool on paper towels, crumble, and reserve. Add the onion to the pan drippings and cook until translucent and just starting to brown, about 5 minutes. Add the teriyaki sauce and honey and stir to combine. Add the reserved beans and bacon and cook, stirring constantly, until sauce coats beans and mixture is heated through. Sprinkle with the toasted almonds. Makes 6 to 8 servings.

CHICKPEA VEGGIE SAUTÉ

I teaspoon	**olive oil**
I	**small zucchini,** cubed
2 cloves	**garlic,** peeled and minced
I can (15 ounces)	**garbanzo beans,** rinsed and drained
I can (15 ounces)	**diced tomatoes,** with liquid
I teaspoon	**Italian seasoning**
¼ teaspoon	**crushed red pepper flakes,** optional
¼ cup	**grated Parmesan cheese**

Heat the oil in a medium skillet over medium-high heat until it shimmers. Add the zucchini and cook, stirring occasionally, until tender and lightly browned, about 5 minutes. Add the garlic and continue cooking for I minute. Stir in the beans, tomatoes, Italian seasoning, and pepper flakes and cook, stirring occasionally, until heated through, about 5 minutes. Sprinkle with Parmesan cheese. Makes 4 servings.

LONG-COOKED SOUTHERN STRING BEANS

I tablespoon	**vegetable oil**
I	**large onion,** chopped
I (8 ounce)	**ham hock**
2 cloves	**garlic,** peeled and minced
I 1/2 pounds	**green beans,** ends trimmed, halved
3/4 teaspoon	**salt**
1/4 teaspoon	**pepper**
1/4 teaspoon	**cayenne pepper**

Heat the oil in a large, heavy saucepan over medium heat until it shimmers and cook the onion until tender, about 4 minutes. Add the ham hock, garlic, and beans. Add enough water to almost completely cover the beans. Bring to a boil, reduce the heat and simmer for I hour. Season with salt, pepper, and cayenne and continue cooking, covered, for I more hour. Remove from the heat and use a slotted spoon to remove the ham hock (use meat for another purpose). Serve the beans accompanied by some of the cooking liquid. Makes 6 servings.

WHITE BEANS AND CABBAGE

2 tablespoons	**olive oil**
1	**medium potato,** diced
1/2	**onion,** minced
1/2 teaspoon	**dried thyme**
1 can (15 ounces)	**white beans,** rinsed and drained
3 cups (1/2 pound)	**finely shredded green cabbage**
	salt and pepper

Heat the olive oil in a large skillet over medium-high heat until it shimmers. Add the potato, spreading evenly in the pan. Cook, stirring occasionally, until potato starts to brown, about 5 minutes. Add the onion and continue cooking until potato is browned and onion is tender, 4 to 5 minutes.

Add the thyme and beans and cook, stirring occasionally, until beans begin to lightly brown, about 5 to 7 minutes.

Stir in the cabbage and continue cooking just until cabbage is tender, 3 to 4 minutes. Season to taste with salt and pepper. Makes 6 servings.

BEST GREEN BEAN CASSEROLE

I pound	**fresh green beans,** ends trimmed
2 tablespoons	**butter**
I	**small onion,** chopped
6 thick slices	**bacon,** cooked and crumbled
$^1/_3$ cup	**mayonnaise**
$^1/_3$ cup	**sour cream**
$^1/_2$ cup	**grated cheddar cheese**
$^1/_4$ teaspoon	**salt**
$^1/_2$ teaspoon	**freshly ground black pepper**

Preheat the oven to 325 degrees and grease a I $^1/_2$-quart baking dish.

Bring a pot of water to a boil, add green beans, and cook for 7 to 8 minutes, or until tender; drain and reserve. In a medium skillet over medium heat, melt the butter and sauté the onion until lightly browned. Add the green beans and bacon and stir. In a small bowl, combine the mayonnaise, sour cream, grated cheese, salt, and pepper. Stir the mixture into the beans and transfer to prepared baking dish. Bake uncovered for 20 minutes, or until heated through and lightly browned. Makes 6 servings.

LENTILS AND RICE WITH FRIED ONIONS

6 tablespoons	**olive oil**
1	**large onion,** sliced
1 1/3 cups	**uncooked green lentils**
1/2 teaspoon	**salt**
3 1/2 cups	**water,** divided
3/4 cup	**uncooked long-grain white rice**
1/4 teaspoon	**pepper**
1/4 cup	**sour cream**

In a large skillet, heat the olive oil over medium heat until it shimmers. Stir in the onion and cook, stirring often, until browned, about 20 minutes. Remove from heat and reserve.

Combine the lentils, salt, and 2 cups water in a medium saucepan over medium-high heat and bring to a boil. Reduce heat, cover, and simmer for 15 minutes. Add the rice and the remaining water to the saucepan. Cover and continue to simmer 15 to 20 minutes, or until rice and lentils are tender. Add half the cooked onions and the pepper into the lentil mixture and stir. Transfer to a serving dish and top with sour cream and the remaining onions. Makes 4 servings.

CREAMY GREEN BEANS AND POTATOES

2 1/2 pounds	**small new potatoes,** quartered
1/4 cup	**butter**
1 pound	**fresh green beans,** ends trimmed
4 ounces	**cream cheese**
1/2 cup	**milk**
1/4 teaspoon	**salt**
1/8 teaspoon	**pepper**

Bring a pot of water to a boil over medium-high heat and cook the potatoes until fork-tender, about 10 to 12 minutes; drain in a colander.

Melt the butter in large skillet over medium-high heat. Add the green beans and cook, stirring often, until tender, about 10 minutes. Transfer the beans to a plate and cover with foil to keep warm.

Add the cream cheese to the butter in the skillet and heat over medium until the cream cheese starts to soften. Lower heat to low and add the milk, salt, and pepper. Whisk the mixture until it becomes smooth and creamy, adding additional milk if needed. Add the potatoes and beans and stir gently to coat with the sauce. Makes 6 to 8 servings.

DESSERTS

FLOURLESS CHOCOLATE CHIP BLONDIES

I can (15 ounces)	**garbanzo beans,** rinsed and drained
$^1/_2$ cup	**natural peanut butter**
$^1/_3$ cup	**maple syrup**
I	**egg**
2 teaspoons	**vanilla**
$^1/_2$ teaspoon	**salt**
$^1/_4$ teaspoon	**baking powder**
$^1/_4$ teaspoon	**baking soda**
$^1/_2$ cup	**semisweet chocolate chips**

Preheat the oven to 350 degrees and grease an 8 x 8-inch baking pan.

Combine the beans, peanut butter, maple syrup, egg, vanilla, salt, baking powder, and baking soda in the bowl of a food processor. Process until batter is blended. Scrape down the sides and process again until batter is smooth.

Fold in the chocolate chips and spread the batter evenly in prepared pan. Bake for 30 minutes, or until edges are lightly browned and a toothpick comes out clean. Cool on a wire rack and cut in 16 squares. Makes 16 cookies.

PEANUT BUTTER AND JELLY THUMBPRINT COOKIES

1 can (15 ounces)	**garbanzo beans,** rinsed and drained
1/2 cup	**natural peanut butter** (creamy or crunchy)
2 teaspoons	**vanilla**
1/4 cup	**honey**
1 teaspoon	**baking powder**
1/4 cup	**rolled oats**
1/4 teaspoon	**salt**
1/2 cup	**jam of your choice**

Heat oven to 375 degrees and line a baking sheet with parchment paper.

Combine the beans, peanut butter, vanilla, honey, baking powder, oats, and salt in the bowl of a food processor. Process until batter is blended. Scrape down the sides and process again until batter is smooth.

With wet hands, roll the dough in 1-inch balls and arrange 2 inches apart on the baking sheet. Press your thumb into each cookie and spoon 1 teaspoon jam in the indentation.

Bake for 12 to 14 minutes, until cookies just start to brown around the edges. Cookies will still be very soft; cool on baking sheet for 5 minutes before removing to cooling rack. Makes about 20 cookies.

SECRET INGREDIENT
CHOCOLATE BROWNIES

1 can (15 ounces)	**black beans,** rinsed and drained
$1/2$ cup	**quick-cooking oats**
$1/3$ cup	**maple syrup**
$1/4$ cup	**vegetable oil**
2 tablespoons	**sugar**
2 tablespoons	**cocoa powder**
2 teaspoons	**vanilla**
$1/2$ teaspoon	**baking powder**
$1/4$ teaspoon	**salt**
$2/3$ cup	**chocolate chips**

Preheat oven to 350 degrees and grease an 8 x 8-inch baking pan.

Combine the beans, oats, maple syrup, oil, sugar, cocoa powder, vanilla, baking powder, and salt in a medium bowl and blend well with an electric mixer until completely smooth. Stir in the chocolate chips and spread into the prepared pan. Bake for 15 to 18 minutes, or until a toothpick comes out clean. Cool for 10 minutes and cut in 12 squares. Makes 12 brownies.

AMAZING CHOCOLATE CHIP COOKIE DOUGH DIP

I can (15 ounces)	**garbanzo beans,** rinsed and drained
1/4 cup	**almond or peanut butter**
1/4 cup	**softened cream cheese**
1/4 cup	**firmly packed brown sugar**
2 tablespoons	**warm water**
2 tablespoons	**maple syrup**
2 tablespoons	**quick-cooking oats**
I tablespoon	**vanilla**
1/4 teaspoon	**salt**
1/8 teaspoon	**baking soda**
1/2 cup	**mini chocolate chips**
	fresh strawberries and graham cracker sticks for dipping

Combine the beans, almond or peanut butter, cream cheese, brown sugar, water, maple syrup, oats, vanilla, salt, and baking soda in the bowl of a food processor. Process until batter is blended. Scrape down the sides and process again until batter is smooth.

Transfer to a serving bowl and fold in chocolate chips. Serve with strawberries and graham cracker sticks. Makes 6 servings.

NOTES

NOTES

NOTES

METRIC CONVERSION CHART

Volume Measurements		Weight Measurements		Temperature Conversion	
U.S.	**Metric**	**U.S.**	**Metric**	**Fahrenheit**	**Celsius**
1 teaspoon	5 ml	½ ounce	15 g	250	120
1 tablespoon	15 ml	1 ounce	30 g	300	150
¼ cup	60 ml	3 ounces	90 g	325	160
⅓ cup	75 ml	4 ounces	115 g	350	180
½ cup	125 ml	8 ounces	225 g	375	190
⅔ cup	150 ml	12 ounces	350 g	400	200
¾ cup	175 ml	1 pound	450 g	425	220
1 cup	250 ml	2¼ pounds	1 kg	450	230